G000268917

Norwegia

Hardanger, Sogne & Geiranger Fjords

Don Philpott & Lindsey Porter

Naeroy Fjord/Aurlands Fjord plus Geiranger Fjord/
Sunnylvs Fjord are on the UNESCO list of Natural &
Cultural World Heritage Sites.

National Geographic nominated the fjords as the best
cared for world heritage area in the world.
It also nominated the fjords as the world's most beautiful
travel destination.

Published by
Landmark Publishing
Ashbourne Hall, Cokayne Ave, Ashbourne,
Derbyshire DE6 1EJ England

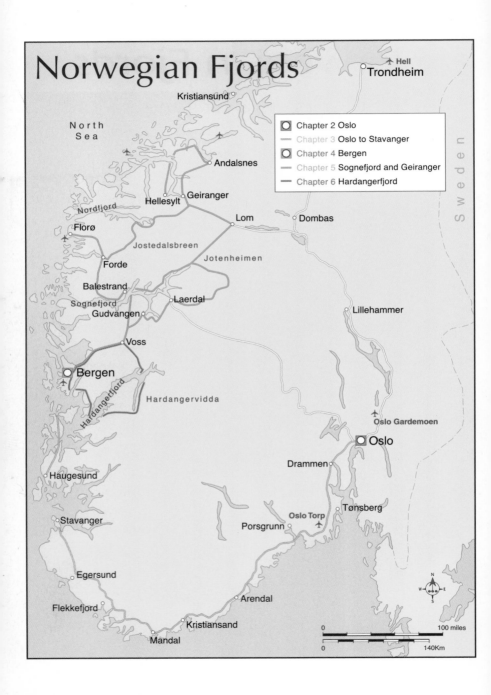

Norwegian Fjords

	Chapter 2 Oslo
	Chapter 3 Oslo to Stavanger
	Chapter 4 Bergen
	Chapter 5 Sognefjord and Geiranger
	Chapter 6 Hardangerfjord

Hell

Trondheim

Kristiansund

North
Sea

Andalsnes

Hellesylt Geiranger

Nordfjord

Lom   Dombas

Florø

Jostedalsbreen

Forde   Jotenheimen

Balestrand

Laerdal   Lillehammer

Sognefjord

Gudvangen

Voss

Bergen

Hardangervidda

Hardangerfjord

Oslo Gardemoen

Oslo

Haugesund   Drammen

Tønsberg

Stavanger   Oslo Torp

Porsgrunn

Sweden

Egersund

N
W   E
S

Flekkefjord   Arendal

0   100 miles

Kristiansand

Mandal   0   140Km

Opposite page: Otternes local museum, Aurlandfjord. (Pål Bugge/Innovation Norway)

Norwegian Fjords

Hardanger, Sogne & Geiranger Fjords

Don Philpott & Lindsey Porter

Published in the UK by
Landmark Publishing Ltd,
Ashbourne Hall, Cokayne Avenue, Ashbourne, Derbyshire DE6 1EJ England
Tel: (01335) 347349 Fax: (01335) 347303
e-mail: sales@landmarkpublishing.co.uk
website: landmarkpublishing.co.uk

Published in the USA by
Hunter Publishing Inc,
130 Campus Drive, Edison NJ 08818
Tel: (732) 225 1900, (800) 255 0343 Fax: (732) 417 0482
website: www.hunterpublishing.com

ISBN 13: 978-1-84306-208-0

ISBN 10: 1-84306-208-9

British Library Cataloguing in Publication Data: a catalogue record for this book is available
from the British Library.

Print: Cromwell Press, Trowbridge
Design & Cartography: Mark Titterton

Front cover: St Olav's church, Balestrand.
Back cover, top: Solvorn.
Back cover, bottom: Hopperstad stave church.

photographs: Uncredited photographs by C.L.M. Porter and R. Morley, p.63.

DISCLAIMER

While every care has been taken to ensure that the information in this book
is as accurate as possible at the time of publication, the publishers and author accept no re-
sponsibility for any loss, injury or inconvenience sustained by anyone using this book.
Maps in this book are for location only. You are recommended to buy a road map (p.106).

The fjords of Norway have a magic and charm all of their own. It is a stunning coastline of constant contrast and change and it would take a lifetime to explore it fully. The magic, however, keeps calling you back. There is the breathtaking scenery of the fjords and open waters, the wonders of the Midnight Sun, beautiful mountains, forests and lakes, bustling towns and sleepy hamlets and the quite magnificent ancient timber buildings. Few sights can compare with the awesome splendour of Geirangerfjord which runs for 10 miles/16km between 4,921ft/1,500m peaks, the majesty of Sognefjord, Norway's longest, the narrow Lysefjord with its sheer mountain sides, and the beauty of Hardangerfjord which reaches 109 miles/179km inland into lush, fertile countryside.

If you are interested in cruising aboard the Hurtigruten (Coastal Express), or motoring and ferry-hopping between the fjords and islands, there is more than enough to offer. The fjords of Norway have a wealth of history, a beautiful countryside, wonderful waterways, plus sunbathing, walking, fishing, reindeer spotting and much, much more. The further north one travels in the summer months, the nearer one is to the sun and temperatures can soar to 30°C (86°F) and higher even in the far north. The air is pure with no filtering pollution and you quickly develop a tan that will be the envy of your friends back home.

This guide sets out to help you make the most of the time you have for your trip. It covers perhaps the most beautiful of the fjords, leading you north from Bergen to visit Sognefjord, Nordfjord and Geirangerfjord before returning to go to Hardangerfjord. It starts, however, in Oslo and describes the route to Bergen, where most British visitors are likely to arrive.

HIGHLIGHTS

Oslo

For its splendid buildings, parks, museums and historic sites.

Bergen

The old town 'Bryggen' with its historic merchants houses, shops, museums and nightlife and Grieg's home nearby.

Trondheim

Historic town and a lively, busy city and port with lots to see and do.

Sognefjord

The 'King of Fjords', stunning vistas with many spectacular ferry trips.

Geirangerfjord

Once visited never forgotten; perhaps the most spectacular fjord in the world.

Hardangerfjord

Especially in early summer when the cherry and apple blossom is out.

GETTING THERE

BY SEA

Getting to Norway from Britain by sea can be a holiday in itself. The North Sea ferries operated by Fjord Line, DFDS Seaways and Smyril Line Shetland are like mini-liners offering excellent restaurants, bars with entertainment, comfortable cabins, sun decks and discos. If you take your own car, you can then motor along Norway's spectacular fjord coast catching ferries where necessary, or take the car on board many of the Hurtigruten coastal steamers which ply between Bergen and Kirkenes in the far Arctic north.

Fjord Line sails from Newcastle to Stavanger, Haugesund and Bergen. **DFDS Seaways** operates from Harwich to Esbjerg in Denmark and you can then take the ferry from Copenhagen to Oslo which sails daily. **Smyril Lines** operates between the Shetlands and Bergen with connecting ferry services to and from Aberdeen operated by Northlink.

BY AIR

There are daily flights by a number of airlines from Britain and other European countries to Oslo and other major Norwegian cities.

British Airways

Operates several flights daily from Heathrow to Oslo.

British Midland

Fly daily between Heathrow, Oslo and Aberdeen.

Norwegian

Operates low-cost flights from London Stansted to Oslo Gardemoen, Bergen and Trondheim. It also offers numerous domestic connection services.

Ryanair

Flies twice daily between London Stansted and Oslo Torp (about 80 miles/130km south of the capital), and daily from Glasgow Prestwick to Oslo Torp.

SAS

Flies daily non-stop from Heathrow to Oslo; and with its partners Wideroe and Braathens from Newcastle to Stavanger and Gatwick to Bergen. It has two daily flights from Heathrow to Stavanger and flies daily except Saturday from Manchester to Oslo. From Scotland it offers four daily flights from Aberdeen to Stavanger and has services from Aberdeen to Bergen.

A LITTLE HISTORY

THE VIKING PERIOD

The Norwegians were great traders and explorers and their skill as boatbuilders had enabled them to produce ships that could sail the oceans. By AD800 the Norwegians had already settled peacefully in Shetland and the Orkneys but the next two centuries were to see a rapid, and not so peaceful, territorial expansion.

Norway was still divided into a number of kingdoms and these joined forces to attack and conquer the Isle of Man, the Hebrides, north Scotland and most of Ireland.

The Vikings settled in parts of England and Normandy, Iceland and Greenland.

The two major events during this period were the unification of Norway and its subsequent conversion to Christianity. Harald the Fairhead defeated the local chieftains in a major sea battle in Hafrsfjord, near Stavanger, in about AD885 and became the first king of a unified Norway. He created 'national' laws which were upheld by nobles appointed to govern the different districts.

Before his death Harald bequeathed the country to his son Eirik, soon to acquire the name of Bloody-Axe, and in doing so established the principle of dynastic rule. He succeeded in having his authority recognised in most parts of the country so that after his death and right up to the union with Sweden in 1319, the kingdom of Norway became an inheritance of the Harald family. This concept of the inherited right of the Harald dynasty took deep root and explains why the royal family is still so highly respected.

The following century Olav Haraldsson (St Olav, Norway's national saint) invited the Catholic Church into Norway and by the time of his death in 1030 much of the country had been converted to Christianity.

It was a period of rapid expansion. In 1066 King Harald Hårdråde was killed at the Battle of Stamford Bridge in a bid to conquer England (this is now regarded as the date that signalled the end of the Viking Age). Harald founded Oslo around 1050, and

Bergen was established about twenty years later. This was the beginning of the great building era when the first of the magnificent timber stave churches were built. Many of the sagas are a record of this period although they embellished the history, merging fact and folklore.

CIVIL WAR AND DANISH RULE

Rivalries between tribal chiefs quickly developed into Civil War and the country was split by intermittent fighting for the next three centuries. Norway's weakness led it to fall prey to the Scandinavian Union of Sweden and Denmark and thereby lose much of its national identity. Many of its trading outposts abroad were taken over by the Hanseatic League and a near fatal blow was inflicted in the mid-fourteenth century when the country was struck by plague.

In 1380 Norway joined a union with Denmark and in 1397, through the Union of Kalmar, Sweden became the third member of the Triple Union. In the 1530s the Union broke up and Norway became part of Denmark, governed by the Danish king. The two countries were often referred to as the 'twin realms'.

In 1537 the Danish king introduced Lutheranism as the official religion of the state and it has remained the State Church ever since. Despite Danish rule and thanks to the relative isolation of much of the country, the Norwegians retained a great deal of their national spirit, culture and language, and were able to develop their own industries. Timber mills and shipyards flourished, iron works were established and the Norwegian middle class grew and began to prosper.

Denmark surrendered large areas of Norway after being defeated by Sweden in the 1640s and 1650s. At the Assembly of the States General in Copenhagen in 1660, Frederik III was acclaimed heir to the throne and given the task of producing a new constitution for the two countries. For the first time Norway was subjected to an absolute monarchy which more often than not was in no position to rule.

FROM THE NAPOLEONIC WARS TO THE PRESENT

Denmark entered the Napoleonic Wars on the side of France, drawing Norway into the fighting alongside her, while Sweden, her former ally, sided against the French. The ensuing continental blockade inflicted enormous damage on Norway's shipping and trade.

Sweden attacked and defeated Denmark and was given Norway in the Kiel peace settlement that followed Napoleon's defeat in 1814. The Norwegians rose up in rebellion. Delegates were elected to a constituent assembly at Eidsvoll, north of Oslo, and on 17 May 1814 they adopted a constitution for a free, independent and democratically governed Norway.

The constitution adopted that day is still in force and is based on three principles – sovereignty of the people, division of powers and inviolable human rights. It provided for a national assembly (the *Storting*) elected by the people with the executive power in the hands of the king who was to elect his government.

The foundation for modern industry in Norway was laid in the 1840s with the establishment of the first textile factories and engineering workshops. The merchant fleet expanded rapidly but there were still hard times.

In 1905 the union with Sweden was peacefully dissolved after a referendum in which the overwhelming majority of Norwegians voted for independence. The Treaty of Karlstad was signed in October that year and Norway became an independent state.

Prince Carl, a member of the Danish royal family, was invited to become king of Norway and he took the name Haakon VII when he ascended the throne in November 1905. The new king became the country's symbol of unity during the construction of independent modern Norway. During the Great War Norway was neutral although the merchant fleet suffered heavy losses because of the submarine war. In 1920 Norway became a member of the League of Nations but the depression hit the country hard and unemployment was severe until the outbreak of World War II.

The German armies attacked Norway in April 1940 and stayed as an occupying power for five years. After two months of war against the much more powerful army, King Haakon VII and his government escaped to London from where they continued the struggle.

The Germans maintained an army in Norway but the Norwegian resistance movement continued to fight them until the country was liberated on 8 May 1945. The king returned to Norway on 7 June 1945 to towns that had been bombed and many northern provinces razed to the ground. The next thirty years saw sustained growth as industry, the merchant fleet, farming, fishing and forestry flourished, helped largely by North Sea oil and natural gas.

The king died in 1957, aged 85, and was succeeded by his only son, King Olav V, who was born in 1903. He married the Swedish Princess Martha (who died in 1954) and had three children, the Princesses Ragnhild and Astrid and Crown Prince Harald, who was heir to the throne. In 1968 the Crown Prince, through a special act of parliament, married Sonja Haraldsen, and on the death of his father in 1991 was crowned King Harald V.

National Independence Day (17 May) is Norway's major national holiday and every year wreaths are laid on monuments and church services are held before the celebrations begin. In every town there are colourful processions led by bands and schoolchildren.

Norway joined NATO in 1949 and was a founding member of EFTA in 1969. The people have twice voted against membership of the EU in referenda held in 1972 and again in 1995, even though the government had successfully negotiated entry.

CLIMATE

The two most surprising aspects of Norway's weather are that it is much milder than one would imagine, and that it can change very quickly. Even in the far north, despite the latitude, one can get a glorious tan during the never-ending summer days. Temperatures between 77°F and 86°F (25°C and 30°C) are not uncommon in northern Norway. There are enormous climatic differences because of the sheer size of the country, but the influence of the warm Gulf Stream, which raises the temperature of the sea, means that even during winter Norway's ports are ice-free. The prevailing, moist westerly winds reach further north in Norway than anywhere else in Europe and deposit a lot of rain, especially in the south and south-west.

The mountains and steep-sided fjords also have tremendous effects on the weather, and one fjord can be enjoying bright sunshine while another nearby is experiencing a downpour. Altitude also affects weather conditions and you can drive from sun-drenched valleys up into thick mist, and then out of it again just as quickly. The coastal climate is less changeable than inland and in the far north. Coastal summers tend to be cooler because of the higher rainfall and accompanying cloud. Bergen can be very wet but the rain clouds can blow away as fast as they arrive and be replaced by beautiful sunshine.

During the summer the days are long and in the north there is permanent daylight. Even in Oslo in midsummer it does not get dark,

11

although the sun ducks down behind the horizon and there are four or five hours of twilight before the very early dawn. The Midnight Sun is a phenomenon only found in areas close to the poles. Because the earth moves on an axis, the northern hemisphere is pointed nearer to the sun during the summer and pointed away during the winter. The most northerly latitudes are closest to the sun in the summer: so close, in fact, that the sun never really sets below the horizon so there is permanent daylight. The exact opposite is the case during the winter, leaving the most northerly latitudes in permanent darkness for much of the time. All places north of the Arctic Circle enjoy permanent daylight on Midsummer Day (23 June) and the further north one travels, the longer this period extends. The best time to see the Midnight Sun is the early season and high summer. The sun does not sink below the horizon at the North Cape from the second week in May until the last week in July.

ARCHITECTURE

The most striking aspect of Norwegian architecture is its use of wood. Timber has been the building material for thousands of years and the Norwegians have perfected the art of creating homes that are both very functional and aesthetically appealing. Ancient farmsteads are still lived in and centuries-old barns (*stabburer*) and other old buildings are faithfully restored.

There are numerous outdoor rural museums throughout Norway containing collections of the oldest houses and barns in the district. As with the Norwegian Folk Museum in Oslo, these buildings were carefully dismantled and then rebuilt on a site where they could be both visited and protected.

It was not until Norwegian Independence in 1814 that there was a sudden increase in demand for new buildings to house the administrators and legislators and this sparked a wave of construction using stone rather than wood. Stone also enjoyed popularity because of the fire risk from timber buildings. The Norwegian love of wood saw a resurgence of timber buildings in the latter half of the nineteenth century and the emergence of the distinctive 'dragon' style, inspired by the secular log houses and stave churches of the Middle Ages. Since the last war the need for urban housing has led to large-scale brick building although the interiors are often finished in wood. Pine-panelled walls, pine floors and elaborately carved pine stairs and banisters can be found in many homes.

STAVE CHURCHES

There are thirty-two of these ancient, magnificent wooden churches left in Norway and all are worth making a detour to see. All are different, both in structure and size. Many are now maintained by the local communities and most are in beautiful locations. Most of these churches were built between 700 and 800 years ago at a time when the rest of Europe was turning to stone for such buildings. The Norwegians, however, had mastered the art of preparing timber that could withstand the ravages of time, and the medieval stave churches still bear witness to this today. They are by far the finest examples of wooden architecture in Norway.

It is only relatively recently that great efforts have been made to protect and restore the remaining stave churches. Although a great deal is known about most of the stave churches, when they were built and their subsequent history, there is still some uncertainty about how their unusual structure developed in the first place. It is suggested that the basic structure, a large wooden hall, was copied from the meeting places used by the chiefs and elders of the Germanic tribes living to the south.

The earliest stave churches were built 'palisade' style. The walls consisted of upright planks buried in the ground. As the technique became more refined at the end of the twelfth century, the Norwegians incorporated many of their shipbuilding methods to construct the stave churches. Four massive corner timber pillars (staves) were erected and the walls were built using hand-hewn wooden planks, which interlocked to give greater strength. The huge planks were here used vertically while on the great longships they were used horizontally. For added strength, cross beams were installed and the roof was added in a series of steps so that the whole structure locked together like a giant cube. Each area of roof was surmounted by an ornately carved cross beam, ending in the shape of a dragon's head, or some other mythical animal. The shingle-clad roofs were very steep to prevent snow compacting. In the later churches, the plank walls in their square timber frame were built on a stone foundation to prevent the wood rotting.

The interior of the church was very dark as there were usually only very small openings high up in the walls. The church interiors, however, contained a mass of ornate carvings. The massive door posts, and often the door itself, were heavily carved with animal and foliage motifs and pagan symbols. Initially the churches would have been plain inside with the altar as the only furniture. As the churches evolved, they were extended, pews were added and internal panelling was painted or carved. In many of the oldest churches there was a covered passage running right round the church – where the men would leave their weapons – and there would have been two entrances, one for men and the other for women.

FLORA AND FAUNA

Norway is rich in trees, and forests cover almost a quarter of the country. The most common trees are spruce, fir and pine, but deciduous trees such as birch are also widespread, and at quite high altitudes.

The vegetation is richest in the southern, south-eastern and south-western parts of the country, regions of dense forests and broad valleys. These valleys often have fast-flowing rivers used by the timber industry to float the logs down to the mills and the sea. This area is also fertile and is the country's main arable region. There are large fruit orchards and cereal farms. Potatoes, other vegetables and fodder crops are grown wherever possible, and well above the Arctic Circle, although the growing season is very short. Crops ripen because of the length of the summer days which makes for almost continuous growth where there is perpetual daylight possible.

The south of the country has a typical temperate central European vegetation while the north has an Arctic flora. On mountain plateaux you can find a vegetation of shrubs, bushes and dwarf trees. The far north has a vegetation mostly of mosses and lichens and ground-hugging plants.

The warmth of the Gulf Stream has led to a rich marine life along the west coast and fishing is import-ant both economically and socially. There is concern, however, that some of the world's richest fishing grounds may have been over-fished in recent years, and government measures have been introduced to try to conserve stocks.

The most important species of fish in Norwegian waters – the eastern North Sea, the Norwegian coast, the Barents Sea and the polar front in the Norwegian Sea – are cod (*torsk*), herring, mackerel, capelin, saithe, haddock, ling, halibut, red-fish, prawns, sprats, squid, blue whiting, sand eel and Norway pout.

The British nobility came to Norway over 100 years ago to fish for salmon. There are about a hundred good salmon rivers, some of them world famous.

Seal stocks seem to be recovering after the mysterious pneumonia-like virus which decimated their numbers on both sides of the North Sea at the end of the 1980s. Walrus can also be spotted in some areas.

On land, the bear is almost extinct while the elk – the Norwegian moose – is mainly found in southern Norway and Trøndelag. In the summer the elk retreat deep into the forests but it is quite common for them to come into towns during the winter as they forage for food.

The reindeer perhaps conjures up the most evocative pictures of Norway. Huge herds still roam the north under the watchful eyes of the nomadic Sami who for centuries have earned their living from rein-deer husbandry. The reindeer usually spend the winter grazing on the vast expanses of the Finnmarksvidda, and are driven to the coast for summer grazing. The largest stock of wild reindeer can be found on Hardanger-vidda. Wild reindeer can still be found in the central mountains, while roe and red deer can be seen in some coastal districts and, less often, inland.

There is great birdwatching throughout the country and many protected reserves, especially offshore islands, which can be seen from the coastal steamers and ferries.

FOOD AND DRINK

The Norwegians take their food seriously and there are many traditional dishes. While there are international restaurants, cafés, burger bars and pizza restaurants in the major towns and cities, traditional cooking still thrives, especially in the countryside, and a meal in a private home is usually a very enjoyable experience.

The Norwegians enjoy an extremely healthy diet and have one of the world's highest consumptions of fish, milk and cheese. They love berries and again there are many special dishes using the various wild berries that can be harvested, which are reserved for particular occasions in the year.

The day starts with *frokost* (breakfast), which is usually substantial as the Norwegians normally have a very light lunch. Porridge is popular, as well as other cereals. This may be followed by smoked fish and cold meats, assorted cheeses, and a variety of breads and jams. Marinated herrings are delicious with brown bread, but one may also be offered crispbreads, including a wafer thin one called *flatbrød*, oatmeal biscuits, potato scones and waffles. Salads may be offered together with fruit juices, milk and coffee. The Norwegians love good coffee and fine tea. It is possible in hotel restaurants and cafés to have a continental breakfast by asking for *kaffe-complet*.

Formiddagsmat (lunch) is usually little more than a snack. It is possible to get a more substantial meal in a restaurant. In cafés and smaller restaurants lunch is usually served up to 4pm and consists of soup, a fish or meat course and dessert. Of course, it is also possible to order à la carte. In larger restaurants and hotels, lunch is generally served from 1pm and a cold buffet is very popular, although this usually includes some hot dishes as well. Open sandwiches are available throughout the day.

Most working Norwegians, however, stop for only about half an hour. They usually have a sandwich of cold meats, fish or cheese and build up their appetite for their evening meal. The large hotels offer both set dinner menus and à la carte, while smaller hotels tend to offer a cold table with a choice of a few hot dishes. The main meal of the day (*middagsmat*) is usually eaten in the early evening.

One of the fascinating things about eating in Norway is that recipes change as you move from one county to another, and every family has a slightly different way of preparing traditional dishes.

Fish is fresh, plentiful and excellent. Salmon (*laks*) and trout (*ørret*) can be served in a number of ways. *Gravlaks* is salmon marinated in dill, sugar, salt and pepper and is usually served with boiled potatoes, or hot potato salad. There is marvellous halibut (*hellefisk*), plaice and sole, crawfish and lobster (*hummer*) in the late summer, and cod (*torsk*), which is served in countless different ways. It is often served

15

with plain boiled potatoes. The Norwegians have learnt not to waste anything: many dishes include fish heads, the liver, which can be boiled and sliced, the roe and the tongue – all now regarded as delicacies.

There is *klippfisk*, which is dried, salted cod; *lutefisk*, cod steeped in potash and a prized delicacy; and *torsk med eggesaus* – cod poached and served with chopped, hard-boiled egg, tomato, parsley and chives.

Other fish to try include eel (*ål*), mackerel (*makrell*), which are often smoked (*røkt*), *rakørret*, which is fermented trout, *rekesaus*, a shrimp or prawn dish in a cream, milk, lemon juice, dill and butter sauce, and herring (*sild*), which is served in innumerable ways. *Spekesild* is salt herring, *skalldyr* shellfish, and *tørrfisk* dried fish. You can also try a Norwegian caviare spread which comes in tubes and is used in sandwiches.

Fiskepudding is ground fish flakes, flour, milk, butter, cream and seasoning, baked in a mould, while *fiskeboller* consists of the same ingredients moulded into fish balls. *Fiskesuppe* is a filling fish soup which may have carrots, parsnips, leeks, potatoes, onion, celery and bay added, and is then thickened using cream and egg yolks. Bergen is famous for its fish soup.

Pork (*svinekjøtt*) is the most popular meat, and pork spare ribs provide the traditional Christmas dinner in most Norwegian homes inland, while *lutefisk* is generally eaten along the coast. Try elk (*elg*) or reindeer (*reinsdyr*) or any of the game birds, such as ptarmigan (*rype*), grouse and capercaillie, which can be served fresh or smoked. There is plentiful mutton, beef (*oksekjøtt*), lamb (*lammekjøtt*), chicken (*kylling*), veal (*kalve*) and venison (*rådyr*).

Betasuppe is a farmhouse mutton soup, and *fenalår* is dried, salted leg of lamb, while *dyrestek* is roast venison, often served with a sauce of goat's cheese and redcurrant jelly. Whole sheep's heads (*smalahovud*) are a great favourite, especially around Voss.

Får i kål is a Norwegian speciality, a stew of mutton and fresh, crisp cabbage seasoned with salt and black pepper. Other meat dishes include *kjøttkaker med surkål*, meat balls with sauerkraut; *kongesuppe*, a thick soup with meat balls, peas, onions and carrots; *lapskaus,* which is a thick stew of chopped meat and vegetables; and *pinnekjøtt*, salt-cured dried mutton ribs traditionally steamed over birch twigs, then roasted and eaten with the fingers. Another treat is *juleskinke*, boiled ham, which is then marinated for two or three weeks.

The Norwegians love warming stews and sausages (*pølser*), and almost any kind of salted, dried or smoked meats. Game is often served with cranberries (*tyttebaer*), and these also figure in a number of desserts. Other desert berries include blue-berries (*blåbaer*), raspberries (*bringe-baer*) and cloudberries (*multer*).

Dravle is a mixture of curds and whey sweetened with syrup; *bløtkake* is a speciality, a cream-filled sponge with fresh fruit or jam and covered in cream; and *eggedosis* is a rich, sweet egg sauce which can have brandy or rum added, and which is eaten alone or poured over bilberries. *Fløtevafler* are waffles made with a sour cream, ginger or cardamom batter; *himmelsk lapskaus* (which means 'heavenly potpourri') is fresh fruit and nuts served with *eggedosis*; and *kransekake* is a cake of layered almond macaroon rings made for special occasions. A very interesting dessert is *lompe*, a pancake made from mashed potato, cream and flour, cooked on a griddle and served with sugar and jam.

There are many different types of cheese made from cow's and goat's milk. Some to watch out for are *gammelost*, which has a sharp taste and an even sharper smell; *gjetost*, a strong, dark brown goat's cheese; *Gudbrandsdalsost*, a lighter, caramel-tasting type of *gjetost* made from a mixture of cow's and goat's milk; *nøkkkelost*, a semi-hard cheese with cloves and caraway seeds; and *pultost*, a soft cheese, sometimes with caraway seeds. *Jarlsbergost* and *ridderost* are very popular cheeses, which are great with bread.

A few words that may be helpful when consulting the menu, or asking for something in a restaurant, are: *brød* – bread, *fisk* – fish, *fløte* – cream, *grønnsaker* – vegetables, *kaffe* – coffee, *kjøtt* – meat, *melk* – milk, *ost* – cheese, *poteter* – potatoes, *regning* – bill, *smør* – butter, *spisekart* – menu, *sukker* – sugar, *te* – tea, *vann* – water, *vin* – wine, and *øl* – beer.

DRINK

Drink in Norway is expensive and at times difficult to come by. All wines and spirits are sold through state-owned shops (*Vinmonopolet*) which can be found in most towns and larger villages. They are heavily taxed and you normally have to join large queues, although the system is very efficient. As you enter the shop you take a number and then wait for that number to come up at one of the serving points.

Beer is good and available in a number of strengths including *pils*, a light lager style, *brigg*, which is almost non-alcoholic, and *bayer*, a dark beer. Export is the strongest *pils* type of beer and *bokkøl* is the strongest dark beer. try the excellent *mackøl* Polar beer, from the world's most northern brewery in Tromsø.

Akevitt is the only spirit produced in Norway. It is not unlike vodka, is drunk neat, usually as a beer chaser, and often accompanies traditional Norwegian food. It is a strong liquor distilled from potatoes, to which herbs are then added.

Alcoholic beer is not always readily available in country areas, and in some shops it has to be ordered for delivery up to a week ahead. Most restaurants and hotels are licensed to sell wine and beer, and the larger hotels will serve spirits as well, but only between 3pm and 11pm outside tourist areas. Measures are about double those in England. On Sundays and holidays hotels and restaurants are not allowed to sell spirits.

Gløgg is a mulled wine traditionally offered by hosts to their guests as they arrive on cold winter nights. It is mulled red wine with cloves, cinnamon and raisins (occasionally fortified with something stronger) and has the power to warm and revive quickly no matter how cold you may be.

Getting Around

By Car

There is an excellent road network around the country although getting from one place to another often takes longer than planned because of the terrain – high mountains and long fjords – and because there is so much to see and do along the way.

Ferries

Ferries make travelling around Norway easier, quicker and more enjoyable. The ferries are remarkably efficient and the timetable enables accurate journey planning. The ferries almost always depart on time, apart from peak periods, and you can normally drive into the terminal as the ferry unloads, then go straight on board.

A short ferry crossing can save hours of driving, and moments spent studying the ferry routes and sailings can help you save time. Many ferries simply help to reduce driving distances, while some routes are worth going out of your way for because of the spectacular scenery to be seen from the boat.

Bookings are only necessary on long-distance ferries although in the height of the season there may be long queues for the most popular ferries and you may have to wait.

There are three major gateways to the Norwegian Fjords – Oslo, Stavanger and Bergen. All are dealt with in this chapter. Our journey starts in Oslo and follows the coast to Stavanger and Bergen. If you are arriving in Stavanger you can pick up the route there. If you plan to arrive in Bergen, you will have to come back another time to do the Oslo–Bergen leg!

2. Oslo

Above: Oslo Harbour.
(Nancy Bundt/Innovation Norway)

Right: Cafe culture, Aker Brygge wharf.
(Johan Berge/Innovation Norway)

HISTORY

According to the old Icelandic chronicler Snorre, Oslo was founded in 1048 by King Harald Hårdråde (Harald the Hard) and he ordered the country's first stone church to be built. The foundations of Gamle Aker church, dating from about 1100, can still be seen in Akersbakken. It is the oldest stone church in Scandinavia and is still used as a parish church.

Oslo became the country's capital when Håkon V chose to be crowned there in 1299. He also ordered work to start on Akershus Castle in about 1300. In the mid-fourteenth century the Black Death hit Norway and the population of Oslo was decimated by the plague. Over the centuries the city has been ravaged by fire many times. After the Great Fire of 1624, the Danish King Christian IV ordered the city to be rebuilt in stone around the castle of Akershus, and renamed Christiania. A permanent exhibition showing how Christiania looked in 1838 is housed at Akershus. In 1694 work started on the cathedral and in 1811 the university was opened. It was during the nineteenth century that Oslo started to flourish again. After being united with Sweden in 1814, the Swedish King Carl Johan XIV ordered a royal palace to be built in the heart of Oslo. It still dominates the city, and there are marvellous views from the royal park down the broad Karl Johans gate.

The city reverted to its original name of Oslo in 1924. The municipality of Oslo covers an area of 169sq miles/454km sq, making it one of the largest capital cities in the world, although much of it occupies wooded hills.

The unmistakable twin-towered City Hall should be your landmark for one of your first ports of call because it is just across from the capital's tourist office, which can supply detailed information about accommodation, organised tours, where to go and what is on. There is a cycle hire shop next door.

If you plan to spend some time in Oslo, you should consider buying the **Oslo Card** from tourist offices, hotels or bus and train stations. It gives free travel on tram, bus, train or ferries, free parking in all municipal car parks, free admission to most museums and other attractions, half price on bus and boat sightseeing tours and special discounts at cinemas. While the cost of the card increases each year, the price is more than recouped by the considerable savings it offers if used fully.

OSLO ATTRACTIONS

City Hall, Rådhusplassen, was started in 1933 but work was interrupted by World War II. It was finally completed in 1950 in time for the celebrations of Oslo's 900th anniversary. The huge red brick structure is dominated by the twin 197ft/60m high towers and was designed by Arnstein Arneberg and Magnus Poulsson. It was agreed from the start that leading Norwegian artists and sculptors would assist in its completion, and the lavish decorations are its major attraction. The building is surrounded by sculptures and contains Europe's largest painting, Henrik Sørensen's *People at Work and Play*, which measures 85ft by 43ft/26m by 13m. It is painted in oil on wood. Other artists involved included Per Krogh, Anne Grimdalen, who created the statue of King Harald Hårdråde on the west wall, and Emil Lie, whose bronze and granite statues are displayed in front of the building. The clock on the east tower measures 28ft/8.5m across, and there is a peal from the 38 bells every hour. There is also a fascinating astronomical clock in the inner courtyard.

Akershus Castle, founded by King Håkon V in 1300, can be reached by walking along the waterfront from City Hall. Although besieged many times it was never taken. The castle was rebuilt by the Danish King Kristian IV after being extensively damaged by fire in the mid-1620s. The fortifications and ramparts were extended, and a Renaissance-style palace built in the middle. During the eighteenth century it was used as one of the country's main prisons, but it then fell into disrepair. During World War II it was used as a political prison and has since been fully restored. The ramparts are open all year, concerts are often held in the chapel on Sundays, and guided tours are available. The State Apartments are now used for official functions. The Royal Mausoleum lies in the crypt beneath the castle's church. The castle also houses the Norwegian **Armed Forces Museum** and the **Resistance Museum**. The former, in what used to be a military arsenal, was opened in 1978 and traces the history of Norway's fighting forces from about 1500 to 1950. The museum has a café, the only one in the area.

Oslo **Cathedral** (*Domkirke*), Stortorvet, was designed by the German architect Chateauneuf and built between 1694 and 1699. It was restored between 1849 and 1850 and again between 1939 and 1950 when it acquired its present interior and new ceiling. The tempera ceiling and monumental decorations depicting scenes from the Old and New Testaments are by Hugo Louis Mohr. The Dutch altarpiece and pulpit date from 1699, and the massive organ facade was created by a Dutch artist in 1727. The new organ, with more than 6,000 pipes, was built by Ludwigsburg and installed in 1930. Emanual Vigeland designed and installed the stained glass windows between 1910 and 1916, and the massive bronze doors, showing the Sermon on the Mount, were created by Dagfin Werenskiold, and installed in 1938.

Basarhallene is next to the cathedral. It was built between 1841 and 1858 and used to be the city's main food retail area. It now sells arts and handicrafts.

Oslo University, Karl Johansgata, was founded in 1811 by King Frederick VI and is Norway's oldest institute of higher education. It was designed by Grist and completed in collaboration with the famous German architect Stinker. The Great Hall contains a number of murals by Edvard Munch.

The **National Gallery**, Universitetsgata, houses Norway's largest collection of paintings and sculptures. Norwegian art from about 1810 is featured with the period of National Romanticism represented by Tidemand and Gude. There are also exhibits from leading European artists such as Rembrandt, Goya and Picasso. Among the many Norwegian artists represented are Christian Dahl, Per and Christian Krohg, Harriet Backer and Jakob Weidemann. Edvard Munch has a separate room devoted to his works. The gallery also houses exhibitions of Danish and Swedish art and a priceless collection of Russian icons.

The **Historical Museum**, Frederiks-

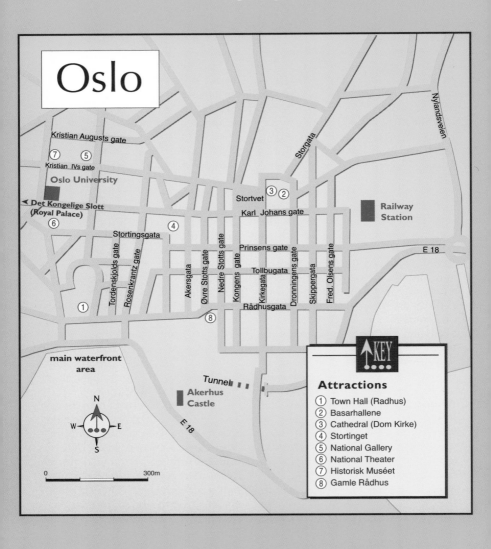

Oslo

Kristian Augusts gate

⑦ ⑤

Kristian IVs gate

Oslo University

◄ **Det Kongelige Slott
(Royal Palace)**

⑥

Stortingsgata

④

Stortvet

③ ②

Karl Johans gate

**Railway
Station**

E 18

Nylandsveien

Storgata

Prinsens gate

Tordenskjolds gate

Rosenkrantz gate

Akersgata

Øvre Stotts gate

Nedre Stotts gate

Kongens gate

Tollbugata

Kirkegata

Dronningens gate

Skippergata

Fred. Olsens gate

Rådhusgata

⑧

①

**main waterfront
area**

Tunnel

**Akerhus
Castle**

E 18

N
W ● ● ● ● E
S

0   300m

KEY
● ● ● ●

Attractions

① Town Hall (Radhus)
② Basarhallene
③ Cathedral (Dom Kirke)
④ Stortinget
⑤ National Gallery
⑥ National Theater
⑦ Historisk Muséet
⑧ Gamle Rådhus

Above: The Royal Palace. *(Nancy Bundt/Innovation Norway)*

Above: The Waterfront with Akershus Castle in the background.
(Kurt Hamann/Innovation Norway)

gate, houses three collec-tions: the University Collection of Antiquities, including the 'Treasury' where the most valuable gold and silver items are kept and medieval ecclesiastical art; the Ethnographic Museum depicting how people live in different parts of the world, along with coins and medals; and the Viking Hall telling the story behind the Viking ships now displayed at Bygdøy.

The **Parliament** in Karl Johans gate was built between 1861 and 1866, although it has been extensively enlarged since. The interior has been richly decorated by contemporary Norwegian artists, and a huge wall painting by Wergeland hangs behind the Speaker's Chair, depicting the 1814 signing of the Norwegian Constitution at Eidsvoll.

The **Royal Palace** stands in its own park at the top of Karl Johans gate. It was built by the Swedish King Carl Christian Johan XIV between 1825 and 1848. The palace is not open to the public, but the park is. The Palace Guard changes at 1.30pm each day, and when the king is in residence the Band of the Royal Guard accompanies the ceremony.

Other museums include the **Museum of Applied Art**, St Olav's gate, which contains the twelfth-century Baldishol Tapestry and a display of royal costumes; the **Museum of Architecture**, Josefinesgate; the **National Museum of Contemporary Art** in Bankplassen; the **Postal Museum** in Tollbugata (first floor); and the **Theatre Museum** in Nedre Slotts Gate, housed in the Old Town Hall.

Sites of special interest include the **Cemetery of Our Saviour**, where Munch and Ibsen are buried; the nearby **Old Aker Church**, the oldest building in Oslo, dating back to the twelfth century, and still a parish church; and the island of **Hovedøya**, a short ferry trip from Vippetangen, at the end of the Akershus promontory. The island was inhabited by Cistercian monks who arrived from England in May 1147. The remains of their monastery can still be seen.

AROUND OSLO

Frogner Park in the north-western suburbs of Oslo is home to one of the world's largest outdoor collections of statues and sculptures, by Gustav Vigeland (1869–1943). His collection started when he was commissioned by the City of Oslo to build a fountain. The result was hailed a masterpiece and a special site was created for it in the royal park. Vigeland was commissioned by the city to produce more statues. Over the next thirty years he produced almost 200 pieces containing over 600 sculptures. He quickly outgrew the palace park site and a new home for his works was found in Frogner Park. You enter the park through his massive wrought iron gates, with their carved animal designs, and the statues stretch out before you in an avenue leading to the spectacular fountain and 65ft/ 20m high monolith, a granite column carrying 121 figures struggling to climb higher. The column is surrounded by 36 groups of statues carved in granite, known as *The Wheel of Life*. The park is open throughout the year and admission is free. The **Vigeland Museum**, in nearby Nobels gate, used to be the sculptor's workshop.

The **Oslo City Museum** is housed in Frogner Manor, which was built about 1790 on the site of a manor which dates back to Viking times. The house contains furnishings from different periods and depicts life in Oslo over the centuries.

Holmenkollen, a short drive out of the city, is Oslo's highest hill and home of the world-famous ski jump and Skiing Museum. There are spectacular views of the capital and the Oslofjord from the top of the jump which is about 1,214ft/370m above sea level. The Skiing Museum is at the foot of the ski jump tower and the galleries housing the exhibits have been excavated into the rock. It is the oldest skiing museum in the world.

Bogstad Manor in Sørkedalen is 6miles/10km north-west of the city, and is regarded as one of the most beautiful houses in Norway. The lakeside house was built between 1760 and 1785 and extended in 1854 and the interior has been well preserved. It has a marvellous art collection and was the first home in Norway to have a landscaped garden.

The **Munch Museum**, in Tøyengata, opened in 1963 and contains all the works bequeathed by the artist Edvard Munch (1863–1944) to the City of Oslo in 1940. The collection contains paintings, drawings, watercolours, lithographs and sculptures. Lectures and concerts are held there. There is a restaurant.

The **Natural History Museum** is in Sarsgate in Tøyen. There are mineral and geological, palaeonto-logical, botanical and zoological museums showing all Norway's animals in their natural habitats, including prehistoric animals and plants. The gardens concentrate on the flora of Scandinavia.

BYGDØY

The **Norwegian Folk Museum** is a magnificent collection of more than 170 old buildings from all parts of Norway. The homesteads and farms, ancient store barns and town houses from the eighteenth and nineteenth centuries are among the trees, and looking down on them is a twelfth-century stave church with fine carvings. In 1885 King Oscar II bought the church from the people of Gol in Hallingdal and had it erected near his summer palace on Bygdøy. Many of the homes have the furnishings and utensils of their period, while others have become workshops where artisans, dressed in traditional costume, practise their crafts of weaving, carving and so on. One building houses Henrik Ibsen's study. A café is open during the summer. Folk dancers and musicians often perform in the grounds.

The **Maritime Museum** has a rich collection of boats housed indoors and also anchored in the bay just outside. Nearby is the Sailors' War Memorial. Outside the museum stands the *Gjøa*, used by Roald Amundsen when he discovered the polar North-West Passage.

The **Kon-Tiki Museum** is across the road from the Maritime Museum, and houses the famous *Kon-Tiki* raft built in 1947 on which Thor Heyerdahl showed that the Polynesians were more likely to

The Munch Museum, Tøyengata, Oslo. *(The Munch Museum Archive)*

be descended from South American Indians than from Asian tribes. The balsa wood raft was copied from the sort of boats used by the Peruvian Indians in AD500. The *Kon-Tiki* sailed the 5,000miles/8,000km from Callao in Peru to the island of Raroia in Polynesia in 101 days. Exhibited with it is the 46ft/14m long papyrus reed boat *Ra II* used in 1970 by Thor and his eight-nation crew for their successful crossing of the Atlantic, and a collection of objects from the Polynesian islands, including several huge carved standing stones from Easter Island.

The **Fram Museum** is next to the Maritime Museum and contains the polar exploration vessel *Fram*, built by Colin Archer between 1892 and 1893 and used by Nansen, Sverdrup and Amundsen on their expeditions to the North and South Poles.

The **Viking Ship Museum** is the most spectacular of Bygdøy's trea-sures. The building was specially designed in the shape of a right-angled cross so that the three Viking ships are displayed to best advantage. All three ships were discovered in the Oslofjord and the finds not only confirmed the remarkable boat-building skills of the Vikings, but gave enormous insight into their culture. The three ships *Oseberg*, *Gokstad* and *Tune* all date from between AD800 and AD900 and were used as burial vessels. Only royalty and the nobility were buried in such fine ships, and the vessels were laden with all the objects of everyday life which would be needed in *Valhalla*.

Oscarshall Castle, overlooking the fjord near the Folk Museum, was built in English Gothic Revival style between 1847 and 1852 as the summer palace of King Oscar I. The walls are decorated by Norwegian Romantic painters.

Above: The Oseberg ship was found in a large burial mound at the Slagen farm in Vestfold and excavated in 1904. The ship was built in around 815-820 A.D. and is now exhibited at the Viking museum, Bygdøy.

(Photographer: Eirik Irgens Johnsen/ © Museum of Cultural History – University of Oslo)

Akershus Castle
☎ 22 41 25 21
Ramparts open: all year. Castle open: May to mid-September, Monday to Saturday 10am–4pm. Sunday 12.30–3pm. Rest of year castle only open Sunday 12.30–4pm.

Museum of Applied Art (Kunstindustrimuseet)
St Olavs gate, Oslo 1
☎ 22 03 65 40
Open: all year, Tuesday to Friday 11am–3pm; weekends 12–4pm.

Armed Forces Museum (Forsvarsmuseet)
Akershus Fortress
☎ 23 09 35 82
Open: all year, Monday to Friday 10am–3pm; weekends 11am–4pm.

Cathedral (Domkirken)
Stortorget, Oslo 1
☎ 23 31 45 00
Open: January to end May and September to end December, Monday to Friday 10am–1pm; June to end August, Monday to Friday 10am–3pm, Saturday 10am–1pm.

City Hall (Rådhuset)
Open: October to end March, Monday to Saturday 11am–2pm, Sunday 12–3pm; April to end September, Monday to Saturday 10am–3pm, Sunday 12–3pm.

Oslo City Museum (Oslo Bymuseum)
Frognerveien, Oslo 2
☎ 23 28 41 70
Open: all year, June to end August, Tuesday to Friday 10am–6pm, weekends 10am–5pm; rest of year Tuesday to Friday 10am–4pm, weekends 11am–4pm.

Frogner Park
North-west suburb of Oslo
Open: all year.
Gamlebyen
Open: throughout the summer (outdoors).

Historical Museum
Frederiksgate 2, Oslo 1
☎ 22 85 19 00
Open: mid-September to mid-May, Tuesday to Sunday 12–3pm; mid-May to mid-September, Tuesday to Sunday 11am–3pm. Closed 1 January, 1 and 17 May, Christmas and Easter holidays.

Munch Museum
Tøyengata 53, Oslo 6
☎ 23 49 35 00
Open: 1 June to 31 August, Every day 10am–6pm; 1 September to 31 May, Tuesday to Friday 10am–4pm, Saturday to Sunday 11am–5pm; Monday closed.

National Gallery (Nasjonalgalleriet)
Universitetsgata 13, Oslo 1
☎ 22 20 04 04
Open: all year Monday, Wednesday, Friday and Saturday 10am–4pm, Thursday 10am–8pm, Sunday 11am–3pm.

Natural History Museum
Sars gate 1, Oslo 5
☎ 22 85 17 00
Botanical gardens May to mid-August, Monday to Friday 7am–8pm, weekends 10am–8pm; mid-August to end September, Monday to Friday 7am–7pm, weekends 10am–7pm; October to end March, Monday to Friday 7am–5pm, weekends 10am–5pm; April, Monday to Friday 7am–6pm, weekends 10am–6pm.

Resistance Museum (Hjemmefrontmuseet)
Akershus Fortress, Oslo 1
☎ 23 09 31 37
Open: October to mid-April, Monday to Saturday 10am–3pm, Sunday 11am–4pm; mid-April to end September, Monday to Saturday 10am–4pm, Sunday 11am–4pm.

Royal Palace (Slottet)
Drammenssveien
Public access to park only.
Changing of Guard daily at 1pm.
When the king is in residence, the
band of the Royal Guard plays
Monday to Friday.

Vigeland Museum
Nobels gate 32, Oslo 2
☎ 23 49 37 00
Open: November to end April,
Tuesday to Sunday 1–7pm; May to
end October 12–7pm.

BYGDØY

Fram Museum
Bygdøynes, Oslo 2
☎ 23 28 29 50
Open: all year, April and November
11am–2.45pm; 1–15 May and
September 11am–4.45pm; mid-May
to end August 10am–5.45pm;
November weekends only 11am–
2.45pm.

Kon-Tiki Museum
Bygdøynesveien 36, Oslo 2
☎ 23 08 67 67
Open: November to end March all
week 10.30am–4pm; April to mid-
May and September to end October
all week 10.30am–5pm; mid-May to
end August all week 10am–6pm.

Maritime Museum
(Norsk Sjøfartsmuseum)
Bygdøynesveien 37, Oslo 2
☎ 24 11 41 50
Open: January to end April and
November to 23 December,
Monday, Wednesday, Friday,
Saturday 10.30am–4pm, Tuesday
and Thursday 10.30am–7pm,
Sunday 10.30am–5pm; May to end
September, all week 10am–8pm.

Norwegian Folk Museum
(Folkemuseet)
Museumsveien 10, Oslo 2
☎ 22 12 37 00
Open: all year.

Oscarshall Castle
Oscarshallveien
Open: mid-May to end September,
Sundays only 11am–4pm.

Viking Ship Museum
Huk Aveny 35, Oslo 2
☎ 22 13 52 80
Open: 01 May to 30 September
9am–6pm; 01 October to 30 April
11am–4pm. Closed New Years Eve,
New Years Day, Good Friday, Easter
Eve, Easter Sunday, Christmas Eve,
Christmas Day and Boxing Day.

3. Oslo to Stavanger

The 372-mile/600km coastal route between Oslo and Stavanger follows the E18 most of the way from the capital, and it is necessary to make a number of detours if you want to see all the things of interest along the way. The south coast is famous for its beaches, ports and resort towns and the roads can be busy in the summer. This route follows the coast road, but if you are cruising along the south coast, it identifies all the main towns and points of interest along the way. Oslofjord runs for 62 miles/100km from the capital to the open sea and the Ferder lighthouse, and the coastline is dotted with picturesque ports, thousands of summer cottages and scores of tiny islands which make it Norway's most popular holiday area.

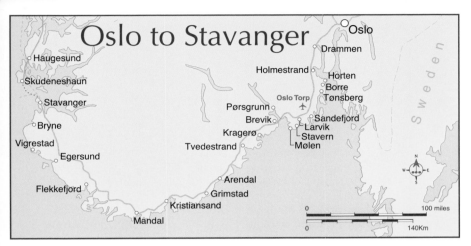

Oslo to Stavanger

Haugesund
Skudeneshaun
Stavanger
Bryne
Vigrestad
Egersund
Flekkefjord
Mandal
Kristiansand
Grimstad
Arendal
Tvedestrand
Kragerø
Brevik
Pørsgrunn
Oslo Torp
Mølen
Stavern
Larvik
Sandefjord
Tønsberg
Borre
Horten
Holmestrand
Drammen
Oslo
Sweden

0   100 miles
0   140Km

If cruising, you pass Oscarsbord, the island fortress built in 1853 to protect Oslo Port. Its two ancient guns, Aaron and Moses, were used to cripple the German heavy cruiser *Blücher* on 9 April 1940, holding up the invasion long enough for the king, other members of the royal family and the government to escape the capital. You also pass the pretty port of Drøbak, which used to act as Oslo's main port during the winter months when ice prevented vessels reaching the capital, and Horten, which until the 1950s was Norway's main naval base.

The fastest way to get out of Oslo is to take the westbound E18, which is clearly signposted to Drammen. It is a toll road but it helps you get out of the Oslo suburbs quickly and is worth the small charge. Not far from Skaugum, the road passes the residence of the crown prince, and there are many turn-offs to the lakes and fjord inlets. **Drammen**, Norway's sixth largest town, is really made up of two towns, Stromsø and Bragernes, which were officially united in 1811, although historians know from rock carvings found that the area has been settled for at least 5,000 years. There is a regional museum, housed in the eighteenth-century Marienlyst Mansion, and an open-air folk museum with many old buildings. Stromsø church was built in 1667 but totally rebuilt in Empire style in the 1840s. The town hall, built in 1872, won an international award in 1986 because of the 'exemplary restoration work'.

If you do not plan to come this way again it is worth making a detour out of Drammen on the toll road to the **Drammen Spiralen**, a 1 mile/1.6km long road tunnel with six corkscrew spirals climbing up through the Bragernesåsen mountain. There is a restaurant at the top and breathtaking views.

If you are interested in art you should detour south to **Hurum** for the **Holmsby Gallery,** home of the Henrik Sørensen collection.

From Drammen the E18 runs through the hills to Sande at the head of Sandebukta, a finger of the Oslofjord, and then along the coast to the charming market town of **Holmestrand**. The sheltered ports have been the home of sailors and shipbuilders for centuries. It was from this coast that the Vikings sailed to Ireland, where they founded Dublin. Holmestrand has been a market town since the eighteenth century and has retained many of its fine old buildings and narrow twisting streets. The town's church, which dates from 1674, has a rare Y-shaped plan, and its museum depicts the town's history and records many of the famous artists who have lived there, including painter Harriet Backer, her sister the composer Agathe Backer Grøndlah, and the author Nils Kjaer.

The E18 continues through **Horten**, a former naval base due to its natural port. The Karl Johansvern base is now the Naval Museum (open daily) and is separated from the town by the Horten canal. The town also has a veteran vehicle museum.

About 1.4 miles/2.5km south of Horten and just off the E18 is **Borre**, with a medieval church, just north of which is Norway's oldest national park containing the largest number of royal burial mounds in Europe. You can take a ferry from Horten for the 30-minute crossing to Moss on the eastern shore of the Oslofjorden.

Next is **Åsgårdstrand**, regarded by the locals as Norway's Paris. Edvard Munch was just one of the many radical artists who lived here and his home, Lykkehuset, is now a museum. The town is an old windjammer port and many of the old homes were built by the merchants and ships' captains.

The next town, **Tønsberg**, is Norway's oldest as well as being the regional capital of Vestfold. Snorre the chronicler recorded that the town existed before the battle of Hafrsfjord which took place in AD872. Because of its sheltered location at the head of a fjord inlet, it was for almost 200 years Norway's most important trading port, but its importance declined because of the proximity of Oslo when it was made the country's capital. During the eighteenth and nineteenth centuries Tønsberg was the base for Norway's whaling fleet. The **Vestfold County Museum** on the western outskirts of town contains collections on the area's whaling and maritime history. The museum opens daily during the summer while the open-air sections are open throughout the year.

Other sights to see include Møllebrakken, an old courtyard just to the south of the city, and Slottsfjellet with the ruins of the thirteenth-century Tunsberghus Castle built by King Håkon Håkonsson. There are excellent views from the top of the hill. There are the ruins of the Church of St Mikael built in 1150, and King Magnus Lagabøter's castle. Sem Church, just to the north of the town, is the oldest in the county and was built in 1100 in Romanesque style.

Many Viking burial mounds have been found nearby, and one excavated in 1917 was the grave of King Bjørn Farmann, who was killed by his brother Eirik Blodøks at the Sem Royal Court in AD933. Also close to the town, just to the north-east, is Oseberg, which gave its name to the Viking burial ship found there, now displayed in the Viking museum at Bygdøy in Oslo.

Sandefjord is a bustling modern town, although it has retained much of its provincial charm. The large, naturally protected bay used to be the world's top whaling port, and the town has the only Whaling Museum in Europe. Apart from the town's impressive whaling statue and fountain, the museum has a 69ft/21m model of a blue whale. The first factory ship sailed to the Antarctic waters to hunt whales in 1905. Today the port exports mainly timber while the major industries are shipbuilding and repairs and light industry.

There are two other museums: the Town Museum, in a house dating from the 1790s, tells the story of Sandefjord, while the Maritime Museum has a fine collection of model ships, pictures and other objects. It was in the northern suburb of Gokstad that the second of the Viking burial ships on display at Bygdøy was found. Sandar church, built in classical style, dates from 1792.

Return to the E18 and head for Larvik, a charming seaside resort between Lake Farris (famous for its mineral water) and Larvikfjord as it starts to open out into the Skagerrak.

The Larvik ferry leaves here to cross to Frederikshavn in Denmark – there are still many important links with Denmark. The Herregaarden, built in 1673–4, was the official residence of the Danish governor of Norway, and today it is a museum. Larvik developed as a whaling station and shipbuilding town – Nansen's vessel *Fram* was built here – but timber and timber exporting are now the major industries. Other things to see include Larvik Old Church, with its painting in the choir by the German artist Lucas Cranach (1472–1553), and the war memorial created by Vigeland standing in front of the new church.

Although the E18 now heads inland along Langangfjorden, it is worth the short detour south to the tip of the **Mølen** peninsula with its lovely beaches, including the famous Oddane Sands, and the nearby Bronze Age burial mounds. Another interesting detour is to **Stavern**, a picturesque seaside resort which used to be one of the country's main naval bases in the 1750s, and still has its eighteenth-century sea defences. There is a rococo church and a war memorial to sailors killed during the First World War. There are many small, attractive seaside resorts along this stretch of coast including Helgeroa and Nevlunghavn.

From Larvik follow the E18 along Langangfjorden to **Porsgrunn**. The town has long been one of Norway's leading ports, and is also now noted as the base for Norway's only china industry, and the home of the multinational Norsk Hydro company, whose nitrate factory is at Herøya. Just up the road is Skien, Ibsen's birthplace, and a little further on at Venstop is the Ibsen museum. The porcelain factory is open to visitors daily. The two churches

Østre Porsgrunn, built in 1760, and Vestre Porsgrunn, built in 1758, both have rococo interiors. The town museum is in an old rectory and the open-air section contains many old buildings with their original interiors. It is open daily but check the times with the local tourist office.

From Porsgrunn the E18 heads south again, through **Brevik**, with its quaint fishermen's cottages, narrow streets and eighteenth-century town hall. Brevik has been a trading port since the sixteenth century. Both the town hall and the old customs house are worth visiting. The road leaves town over the 148ft/45m high, 2,221ft/677m long bridge spanning the Brevikstrømmen, through the small port of Stathelle on the west bank, and into the district of Sørlandet, noted for its many seaside resorts and charming coastal towns.

Next is **Kragerø**, one of a cluster of communities known as the 'white towns'. Kragerø is now a very fashionable resort with its old timbered houses and narrow, winding streets. The town museum is at Berg 7miles/4km away, surrounded by marvellous gardens.

Visit the batteries at **Gundersholmen**, used to repel English warships during the Napoleonic wars. There are many small offshore islands to visit, and boats can be hired, or you can take one of the many organised trips. Just off the main road is **Sannidal**, with a church dating back to 1771 but incorporating the porch from a medieval stave church.

Risør is another delightful resort with its well-preserved wooden houses nestling around the port. The town is one of the oldest on the south coast, and has been a port since 1630. The Church of the Holy Ghost dates from 1646 and is a fine example of baroque cruciform style with ornate carvings and paintings. Søndeled church, originally built in stone about 1150, has a fine old tapestry. The Kastellet Citadel by the port was built at the beginning of the nineteenth century, and the Risørflekken is one of the oldest navigation aids along the south coast and can be seen from more than 12miles/19km out at sea.

Risør is famous for its beaches, the many small offshore islands to explore, and the summer regattas which culminate in the Wooden Boat Festival. An art exhibition is held in the town all year round, and the town has its own 'watchman' whose job is to patrol the older parts of the town and offer information to visitors. Risør also boasts the largest pothole in northern Europe, known as the Whirlpool.

Tvedestrand, although a popular summer resort, earns some of its income from making Christmas decorations, and there are a number of cottage industries producing dried flowers. *Strykejernet* ('the iron') in Tvedestrand is thought to be Norway's narrowest house. The town is built round the old iron works (Nes Verk) where some of the oldest workmen's homes in Norway are to be found, dating back to 1738. The large wooden town hall by the port is now an art gallery and you can watch craftsmen at work there, including glassblowers. The former defensive outer port can be seen running from island to island offshore. Tvedestrand has some marvellous fish restaurants. A short distance west of the town is Holt, whose medieval church was enlarged to a cruciform church in 1753.

Arendal was granted its charter in 1610 and was a major shipping port in the late Middle Ages because of its large, well-protected port. Last century more than 100 sailing ships were registered in the port, and hundreds more used it. Today the boats do not go quite so far afield but there are many sightseeing trips organised around the numerous offshore islands. The old town (Tyholmen) is very well preserved with its old, brightly painted wooden houses. It was once called the Venice of the north because canals used to link many parts of the old town, but these were eventually drained and became streets.

The town hall is one of Norway's tallest wooden buildings, built in Empire style around 1812–14. Trinity Church, built in 1888 and the largest in the county, has a musical tower almost 295ft/90m tall, which plays choral works during festivals. The old battery overlooks the port, and the museum is on the nearby island of Merdøy, and has been arranged to resemble an old sea captain's home. There are some marvellous fish restaurants.

Grimstad has been a port since 1791 and is now famous for its fruit preserving and fruit wine industries. It is the region's major cultural town and the art association stages exhibitions, plays, films and concerts during the year. The many offshore islands used to afford protection to the sailing ships in the nineteenth century which is why the port became so popular. Many of the houses today were owned by seafarers, and retain their original charm.

Things to see include the Town Museum. Once a chemist's shop, it was Henrik Ibsen's home for a time. The museum has the world's largest collection of Ibsen manuscripts, as well as a large collection of maritime exhibits. Ibsen also lived between 1844 and 1850 in what is now the art gallery, which is open all year. During June and July special exhibitions are held. Just outside the town is the eleventh-century Fjaere stone church where Terje Vigen of Ibsen's famous poem is buried.

At **Nørholmen** you can visit the home of author Knut Hamsun, bought with his Nobel Prize money in 1918. The town hosts an annual film festival. The road then arrives at **Lillesand**, a small town with a long trading history and a wide variety of architectural styles reflecting its international character. During the eighteenth and nineteenth centuries its traders visited England, Scotland and France and the styles of these countries can be found among the old houses around the port. One of the finest examples is the estate of merchant Carl Knudsen, built in Empire style in 1827 and now the home of the town and maritime museums. The town hall, dating from 1734, won an international award for its restoration in 1984. The medieval stone Vestre Moland church was extended to a wooden cruciform in 1797. If you have time, take one of the many boat trips.

Continue along the E18 to **Sørlandsparken**, which contains the **Dyreparken Zoo**, a trotting course and amusement park. It is the biggest attraction in the area and Norway's only zoo. It is 7miles/ 12km out of town, just off the E18, and reached by crossing the 1,968ft/ 600m long Varrord Bridge, one of the longest in Scandinavia. The 40-hectare (100-acre) zoo, funfair and activity park have more visitors than any other attraction in Norway.

It is then a short drive to Kristiansand.

Kristiansand is the capital of south Norway, and the country's most important ferry port linking it with Hanstholm and Hirtshals in Denmark, and Amsterdam. There are several sailings daily. It is serviced by the airport at Kjevik, just to the north of the town.

Apart from its bustling port, the first thing that strikes you as you explore the town is its chessboard layout, a legacy of Denmark's King Christian IV who planned it in 1641 and gave it its name. This oldest part of town is known as Kvadraturen. It flourished in the nineteenth century both as a port handling the ocean-going sailing ships and windjammers, and as a shipbuilding port, but the real growth has been this century because of industrial development. Although now the 'holiday capital' of Sørlandet, at the heart of the Norwegian riviera, Kristiansand is an important industrial town with its port and factories. The Christiansholm Fortress, dating from 1674–9, stands beside the eastern port and today houses an arts and cultural area, and a delightful restaurant. The

walls of the rotunda are 16ft/5m thick.

There are also interesting art collections in the Billedgalleriet; the **Vest-Agder County Museum**, an open-air museum with more than thirty fine old buildings, as well as church fixtures and town and country furniture and costumes; and the **Arne Vigeland Museum**, with its bronze and plaster sculptures, on the nearby island of Lagmannsholmen. The **Kristiansand Museum**, Gimlegården (open daily except Monday), shows the cultural history and natural history of the area and is set in beautiful parkland. The **Monte Carlo Bilmuseum**, next to the zoo, has a collection of old and luxury cars.

The Gothic cathedral with its 230ft/70m high tower, Norway's third largest, was built in 1885 and can seat 1,800 people. The previous cathedral was destroyed in a fire. The Oddernes church, built about 1040, has a baroque pulpit dating from 1704, and an interesting rune stone outside. The rose-painted interior of the wooden Søgne church is also worth inspecting.

Mandal is Norway's most southerly town and one of its most picturesque. It is the oldest of the towns along the south coast and the old town, with its white painted wooden houses, has retained all its charm. The town sprawls on either side of the estuary of the Mandal river, the oldest quarter is built round the marketplace and the finest of the old houses are found in Store Elvegaten. The parish church, built in Empire style in 1821 and capable of seating 1,800 people, is Norway's largest wooden church. The Skrivergården was built in 1776 in the style of a Scottish country house, and is now the town hall. The town museum and art gallery is housed in Andorsengården, which was built in 1801, and there is a statue by Gustav Vigeland, who was born in the town.

Other interesting buildings include the Hald Summerpension which was built in 1795 and 'moved' to Mandal on board the sailing vessel *Caledonia* in 1899, and Risøbank, the old summer residence of Lord Salvesen. It was built in 1901 and the house, now a museum, is preserved in its own parkland. The open-air folk museum has a beautiful rose-painted store-house and is open from 10 June to 10 August.

There is a charming 100-hectare/ 250-acre nature park, Skernjøy, open daily with maple walks running down to a one-mile (2km) stretch of coves and beaches, the Sjøsanden.

After leaving Mandal head for **Kvinesdal**, a town nestling at the head of Fedafjord. The Utsikten Hotel also houses the local museum, and is a good vantage spot for viewing the fjord.

The next town is **Flekkefjord**, an attractive settlement almost surrounded by hills and with a well-protected port. The town straddles the river and is sandwiched between the hills and Flekkefjord to the south-east and Grisefjord to the north-west.

The old town is still known as Hollenderbyen (Dutch Town) because its principal trade in the 1820s and 1830s was shipping timber to Holland. Some of the oldest houses were even built in Dutch style and you can wander round the narrow, twisting lanes and view them and the boathouses fronting the water. Today the major industries are fishing, tanning and furniture making. The town's octagonal wooden church was built in 1833, and the museum is housed in a local dignitary's home built around 1720.

Egersund is the next destination along coastal highway 44. The route cuts through tunnels and past beaches and more charming little resorts, such as the fishing village of Åna-Sira.

You can take a detour up the twisting road to the summit of the ridge overlooking Jøssingfjorden, scene of an heroic rescue during World War II. On 16 February 1940, boarding parties from the British Royal Navy destroyer *Cossack* stormed the anchored *Altmark*, a German merchantman, being used to hold 300 British seamen prisoners of war.

Egersund is a market town whose prosperity was built on its herring fishing and processing industry last century, and fishing is still its mainstay. There are many lovely old wooden homes, especially along Strandgaten, and during the summer there are direct ferry links with Hirtshals and Hanstholm in Denmark. Egersund church was built in 1605 and rebuilt in cruciform style during the eighteenth century. The altarpiece dates from the beginning of the seventeenth century. Also visit the Dalane open-air folk museum in the northern suburb of Slettebo. Take the 44 out of town to find it. You can also take a side trip down to the lighthouse at Eigerøy, and the safe bathing beaches at Eigerøya.

For a while the road runs alongside the North Sea, and this stretch of highway is known as Nordsjøveien. Stop and visit the ancient Evestad burial ground at **Vigrestad**, and then on through Bryne, home of the national dairy college, to Sandnes and the E18 for the short drive north to Stavanger.

If you want to explore around **Bryne**, there are some wonderful beaches, especially those on Jaerens Reef which are also popular with bird watchers. The coast road which bypasses Bryne is highway 507 which turns off from highway 44 at Søyland. At Bore it connects with highway 510 which runs into Stavanger. The 507 passes through **Orre**, with its fifteenth-century church, and many good beaches.

Stavanger is an oil boom town. It has grown enormously in the last few years and is now the fourth largest town in Norway. The southern approach to the town now consists of a long drive through industrial and residential areas. The sea has always played an important part in the town's 850-year history. It was a trading post in the eighth century, but its fortunes blossomed in 1125 when work started on the cathedral. The large North Sea ferries are dwarfed as they sail past the massive oil rigs under construction or repair in the port, and many of the town's newest and most modern buildings have been built by the oil companies and the industries servicing them. The tourist office is next to the railway station and, apart from a wealth of local information, it also has details on how and where to hire bikes.

The Stavanger Card is useful if you plan to spend some time in the town. You can buy it when registering at your hotel, guesthouse or campsite, or in advance, through Stavanger Tourist Office. It gives 50 per cent off museum entry, railway and bus travel, concerts and some sports facilities, and smaller but still significant discounts off boat trips, cinema and theatres and so on.

Stavanger Cathedral is across the road from the market square and between Haakon VII's gate and the Breiavatn lake. It was built on the orders of King Sigurd the Crusader, when he made the town a Bishopric in 1125. Bishop Reinald from Winchester was in charge of the building work, and many English craftsmen were recruited. The cathedral is dedicated to St Svithun, and was originally built in Anglo-Norman style. After being damaged by fire in 1272, the chancel was rebuilt in Gothic style and completed in 1300. It is the only medieval cathedral in Norway to have retained its original style.

Kongsgården, beside the cathedral, was built in the thirteenth century and was originally the Bishop's Palace. The Mauke Chapel was subsequently added. The palace was taken over as one of the Danish–Norwegian royal residences and then became the home of the district governor. To the north of the market square is the Valberg Tower, a former watchtower, which now gives visitors an excellent view of the town, fjord and mountains.

Ledål Manor is a mansion built in 1800 for the wealthy Kielland family and restored with furnishings

Above and below: Stavanger waterfront.

of that period. It is the official royal residence when the king or members of the royal family visit the area.

The **Maritime Museum**, in Nedre Strandgate, has exhibits showing the town's maritime development over the last 200 years from sail to oil.

Old Stavanger around **Øvre Strandgate** is the best preserved old quarter of wooden houses in northern Europe. The 150 or so houses are all in a conservation zone and are inhabited. The houses all date from the end of the seventeenth and beginning of the eighteenth centuries, and are remarkably well maintained.

The **Canning Museum**, in Øvre Strandgate, is a reconstructed sardine canning factory dating its heyday between 1890 and 1920.

Stavanger Museum, in Muségaten, contains cultural and zoological exhibits. It shows Rogaland's flora and fauna from the sea to the mountains, as well as the region's arts and crafts.

Vestlandske Skolemuseum in Hillevåg is in the old Kvaleberg school, and has a collection of old and new educational equipment, and a large library of educational books which can be borrowed. **Stavanger Botanical Garden** is at Ullandhaug. Stavanger has a rich cultural life with many galleries, theatres and concert halls. The **Stavanger Art Gallery** has a fine collection of paintings by Norwegian artists, including Stavanger's most famous artist Lars Hertervig. The **Stavanger Concert Hall** at Bjergsted is the home of the Stavanger Symphony Orchestra.

Utstein Kloster (check the opening times with the local tourist office) on the island of Mosterøy is Norway's best-preserved abbey and cloisters from the Middle Ages, and attracts about 30,000 visitors a year. It has also been a royal residence and a manor house. Mosterøy and the adjacent island of Rennesoy are reached by a long undersea tunnel which forms part of the E1 route from Stavanger to Bergen.

Other trips include Mosvanns Park with its rich wild bird life, the telecommunications tower at Ullandhaug for its spectacular panoramic views, and a day tour along Lysefjord to the **Prekestolen** (Pulpit Rock). It is quite a difficult climb to the top of the huge slab of rock with its sheer cliff sides. The top is 1,968ft/600m above sea level.

There are many beaches in the area but the nearest is at **Sola**, famous for its white sand.

An exciting day trip is to take the ferry from Stavanger to **Lysebotn** and enjoy some of Norway's most spectacular fjord scenery. The steep mountain walls were carved out by glaciers during the Ice Age, and in many places the fjord is as deep as or deeper than the mountains towering above you. From Lysebotn, drive into the mountains heading for Sirdal, Sørlandet's answer to the Troll Path. The mountain has 32 hairpin bends and in places sheer drops of more than 2,624ft/800m and more. The climb is worth it, however, as the scenery opens out with spectacular heather moors and a background of mountains.

STAVANGER TO BERGEN

The coastal strip in the north of Rogaland is a mixture of grassland and marsh. There is a galaxy of islands to explore, especially Karmøy, which can be reached by ferry, or by island hopping, from Sand for example. Rogaland also enjoys a very pleasant climate thanks to the warming influence of the Gulf Stream.

Getting around Rogaland poses no problems despite all the fjords because of the ferries. Some routes can be very busy at peak times, such as the Rennesøy to Skudeneshavn on Friday afternoons, and vice versa on Sunday evenings. If you are planning a lengthy stay on the Ryfylke islands, it is a good idea to take bicycles with you, or hire them, because they are certainly the best way of getting around. You can hire cycles through the tourist office in Stavanger or at one of the many cycle hire shops in town.

From Stavanger you can ferry hop and see the western islands, or you can hug the coast along the eastern shores of Sørfjorden as far as Kinsarvik where you catch the ferry across to Kvanndal (45 mins). From here you drive westwards for about 87 miles/140km into Bergen. It is possible to catch a ferry direct from Stavanger to Bergen and beyond and this is dealt with in the next section.

There are many options for getting out of Stavanger. You can ferry to the island of Karmøy and then island hop, seeing Haugesund, Leirvik and Osöyro. You can catch a ferry through the islands of Ryfylke

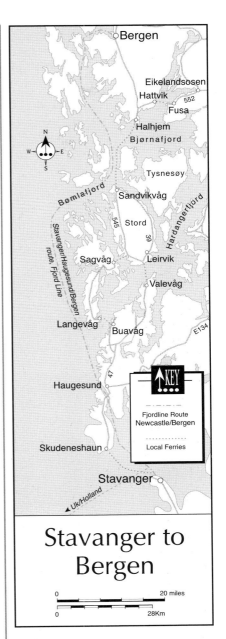

Stavanger to Bergen

The Karmsund Bridge, on the Stavanger-Haugesund seaway.

Haugesund.

as far as Sand where you pick up the highway and travel north via Odda, Brimnes and Voss to Bergen. The other alternative is to drive south out of Stavanger to Sandnes and then pick up highway 13 to Lauvvik for the short ferry hop across to Oanes. This route takes you along the coast through Hjelmeland to the Hjelmeland–Nevsik ferry across Jøsenfjorden and then north to Sand.

Once you have got used to hopping on and off the ferries, you may feel like detouring from Sand to visit Haugesund and Kopervik or any one of the charming communities that can be discovered on the western islands.

The road hugs the coast because to the east the mountains climb rapidly and for most of the year are impenetrable. There are a number of small roads running inland but it is best to seek advice from the locals about whether your vehicle is suitable to use them.

BERGEN VIA KARMØY

The ferry from Rennesøy takes about 50 minutes to cross over to **Skudeneshavn,** on the southern tip of the island of Karmøy, which used to be the seat of the Norwegian kings in the early Middle Ages. Skudeneshavn is one of the most picturesque port tours on the west coast and developed in the seventeenth century because of the rich lobster fishing in the area. More recently its prosperity depended on the herring fisheries. The old part of town is known as the Empire Quarter because of the style of architecture which predominates.

There is also an interesting park which has been planted with trees from around the world.

From Skudeneshavn you can drive either along the island's western coast on highway 47 which looks out across the North Sea, or along highway 511 which follows the more sheltered eastern coast looking out to Boknafjord.

There are a number of beaches along both coasts but the highway 47 route is more dramatic, taking you through the fishing village of Sandve and the beach complex with camping site and cabins for hire at Sandvesanden. There is also a youth hostel here. Åkrehamn is another fishing village but rather special because of its massive sea defences needed to protect it from the fury of North Sea storms.

Åkre church dates from 1821 and has a very old altarpiece. This area is one of the most popular bathing spots and the beach at Åkresanden stretches for more than a mile (1.6km).

The road then crosses the island with highway 511 merging with it just north of Kopervik, a major pilot station. There is plenty of accommodation in the area from hotels and guesthouses to campsites and cabins (*hytte*).

Continue to Avaldsnes, famous for its church built in 1250 and the Virgin Mary's Needle which stands nearby. According to legend, the world will end on the day that the slightly tilting 21ft/6.5m tall stone touches the wall of the church.

At Bø there are Stone Age burial mounds, and at Rehaugene a number of ancient monuments from the Bronze Age can be seen. You leave the island on the 2,263ft/690m long Karmsund Bridge which is 213ft/65m above the water, and affords magnificent views all around. After crossing the bridge you will spot five standing stones, known as the Five Foolish Virgins. The reason for their name is not known, but the stones have been standing there since the Iron Age.

Continue into Haugesund, a very old settlement. Although it did not receive its town charter until 1854, the settlement has played a long and distinguished role in Norway's history.

Haugesund is now a modern fishing and shipping port, one of the largest in Norway. It is also internationally famous for its annual North Sea Festival, which attracts anglers from all over the world, and as the venue of the Norwegian Film Festival. The town hall is worth visiting and there is a very interesting museum. Every day during the summer there are fishing trips organised by the local tourist office.

Just over one mile (2km) to the north of the town is **Haraldshaugen**, the grave of Harald Hårfagre (Harold the Fairhair), one of the most famous of all the Viking kings, and responsible for uniting Norway. In 1877, a 56ft/17m tall granite obelisk was erected on the site and it is now a national monument. The obelisk is surrounded by twenty-nine stones, one for each of Norway's different districts at the time of unification. Close to the south of the site is Krosshaugen, an early meeting place of the *Thing* (the Assembly for Lawmaking and Legal Judgements) with a stone cross dating back to AD1000.

From Haugesund you take the 11 or highways 47 and 1 to Valevåg if you want to continue island hopping. The ferry takes you to the island of Stord where you can break your journey for bathing or walking. There are a number of campsites on the island, many good beaches and some good hills to climb, including Midtfjell (1,624ft/498m), Kinno (1,863ft/568m), St Melen (1,640ft/500m) and Kattnekken (2,375ft/724m). **Leirvik**, on the south-east coast of Stord, is a product of the oil boom. Although a long-standing ship-building area, its fortune was transformed after the discovery of North Sea oil and most of its activities are now oil related. There is a large Bronze Age burial site at Fitjar on the north-west coast of the island.

From Sandvikvåg on the northern tip of Stord you can ferry across to either Huftarøy, which is connected by bridge to the island of Selbjørn, or direct to Halhjem (60min) on the mainland, about 16 miles/26km south of Bergen on highway 47.

An interesting detour from Stord is to take the ferry to the island of **Moster**, west of Rennesøy, and visit Norway's oldest stone church, built by Olav Tryggvason in AD995.

Holmsbu Gallery
Home of the Henrik Sørensen Collection. Between Holmsbu and Rødtangen.

Vestfold County Museum
Exhibits on the area's whaling and maritime history. Open daily during the summer. Open air displays open year round.

Dyreparken Zoo
Norway's most popular attraction. A 40 hectare (100 acre) zoo, funfair and activity park. Open year round 10-3, later in the summer.
☎ 38 04 98 00

Vest-Agder County Museum
Open air museum with more than 30 old buildings as well as old church fixtures, town and country furniture and clothing. Open year round.

Arne Vigeland Museum
Famous for its bronze and plaster sculptures. Open Mon to Sat 10-6, Sun 12-6.

Kristiansand Museum
Exhibits on the cultural and natural history of the area. Set in beautiful parkland. Open daily except Sunday.

Monte Carlo Bilmuseum
Sorlandsparken, close to the zoo. Collection of old and luxury cars. Open year round 12-3 but times may vary.
☎ 38 04 16 59

Stavanger Art Gallery
Madlaveien. Fine collection of paintings by Norwegian artists including Stavanger's most famous artist Lars Hertervig. Open Sept to May Mon to Fri 9 to 2 and 6-8, Sat 12-3, and Sun 12-5.
☎ 51 52 04 63

Ledål Manor
Eiganesveien. Royal residence and manor house museum. Newly restored. Open year round except Sundays in December and January.
☎ 51 84 27 00

Maritime Museum (Stavanger)
Nedre Standgt 17 & 19. Exhibits depict the development of shipping, shipbuilding and commerce over the past 200 years. Playshop for children. Open 11-4pm.
☎ 51 84 27 00

Stavanger Museum
Muségate 16. Historical tableaux depicting scenes from Stavanger's 870 year history and flora and fauna exhibits from throughout Norway. Open 11-4 although times may vary.
☎ 51 84 27 00

Stavanger Botanical Gardens
Rektor Natvig Pedersenvei 40. Beautiful gardens open year round. Café.
☎ 51 50 78 61

Vesandske Skel Museum (Stavanger)
Hillevåg. Interesting educational exhibits and extensive library in an old Kvaleberg School. Open year round although times vary.

4. Bergen

Bergen, the fjord capital of Norway, is one of the most beautiful cities in the northern hemisphere, surrounded by mountains and fjords. Bergen is famous for its music and drama and its annual international festivals. It has one of the world's oldest symphony orchestras and a fine theatre. There are old buildings, cobbled streets, markets and parks to explore.

Take the funicular railway to the summit of Mount Fløien 1050ft/ 320m or the cable car up Mount Ulriken 1968ft /600m. From either you can see Bergen spread out beneath you, with its massive natural anchorage on which its prosperity was built, and the fjord reaching through the mountains to the sea. Bergen's tourist offices have a wealth of information and there are daily guided tours of the city, as well as scores of other sightseeing trips available.

Bergen became a city during the reign of King Olav Kyrre (Olav the

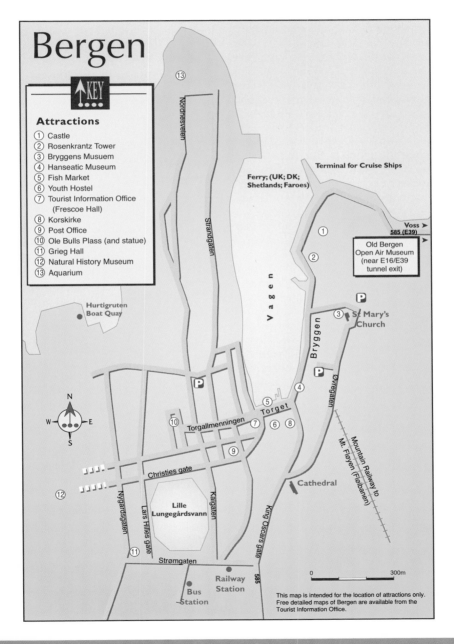

Bergen

KEY

Attractions

1. Castle
2. Rosenkrantz Tower
3. Bryggens Musuem
4. Hanseatic Museum
5. Fish Market
6. Youth Hostel
7. Tourist Information Office
   (Frescoe Hall)
8. Korskirke
9. Post Office
10. Ole Bulls Plass (and statue)
11. Grieg Hall
12. Natural History Museum
13. Aquarium

Terminal for Cruise Ships

Ferry; (UK; DK; Shetlands; Faroes)

Voss ►
585 (E39)

Old Bergen
Open Air Museum
(near E16/E39
tunnel exit)

Nordnesveien

Strandgaten

Vagen

Hurtigruten
Boat Quay

Bryggen

St Mary's
Church

Ovregaten

Torget

Torgallmenningen

Christies gate

Nygardsgaten

Lars Hilles gate

Kaigaten

Lille
Lungegårdsvann

Cathedral

Mountain Railway to
Mt. Floyen (Floibanen)

King Oscars gate

Strømgaten

585

Bus
Station

Railway
Station

0   300m

This map is intended for the location of attractions only.
Free detailed maps of Bergen are available from the
Tourist Information Office.

Peaceful, 1066–93), although records show that it was the site of a much older trading post. Its large natural anchorage meant it quickly grew as a fishing and trading port. In the twelfth and thirteenth centuries Bergen was Norway's first capital and it remained Scandinavia's largest port and trading point throughout the Middle Ages. Hanseatic merchants had their houses along one side of the quay and today they provide a living museum, an elaborate network of wooden buildings with pointed gables, narrow alleys and cobbled courtyards leading to the workshops and warehouses behind.

Bergen is a major education city with its university and several colleges, and is the cultural heart of the region. The Bergen Philharmonic Orchestra was founded in 1765 and the country's first permanent theatre was built in 1850. The most important cultural event is the International Festival of Music, Drama and Folklore held annually at the end of May and beginning of June, which is world famous.

The **Bergen Card** entitles you to discounts / free admittance to many places; free bus travel within the city limitsetc. Available from the Tourist Information Office in the Fresco Hall, Railway Station and Express Boat terminal.

BERGEN ATTRACTIONS

You can explore the **Torget**, the famous fish market, which stands at the head of the inner quay, Vågen. The market not only sells fish, but fruit, vegetables and flowers. It is open daily, except Sunday, 8am–6pm.

Bergenhus Fortress (Bergen Castle) grounds contain some of Norway's most famous medieval buildings. Håkon's Hall was built by King Håkon Håkonsson between 1247 and 1261 as the largest and most imposing building in the royal residence in Bergen. There are guided tours of the Great Hall where Norway's kings were crowned, and Rosenkrantz Tower. It is used as one of the spectacular venues for the International Festival.

Rosenkrantz Tower was built in the 1560s by Erik Rosenkrantz, the Governor of Bergen Castle, as a combined defence and residential tower. It incorporates two much older structures, King Magnus the Lawmender's keep from about 1260 and Jørgen Hannsøn's outwork from about 1520. The Fortress and Tower were badly damaged when a ship blew up, but both have been carefully restored.

Bryggen is a wonderful collection of wooden buildings facing the quay, and to the west of the Torget market. It gets its name from *tyskebryggen*, which means 'docks' or 'quays' in German, and is now recognised by UNESCO as a World Heritage Site. The protected old Hanseatic buildings now house shops, restaurants, artists' studios and workshops where painters, weavers and other craftsmen work. Many of the studios are open to the public.

The buildings were erected in 1702, after a fire destroyed virtually the whole of Bergen. The right-hand half of Bryggen was demolished about 100 years ago and replaced by the taller, stone buildings to be seen today. The left-hand building of this block incorporates a tower. Notice the German double-headed eagle on the gable, recalling the former Hanseatic League connection. The building at the right-hand end of the row is the Hanseatic Museum, established in 1872.

St Mary's Church (Mariakirken), to the north of Bryggen, is the oldest building in Bergen and one of the outstanding Romanesque churches in Norway. It was built in the first half of the twelfth century and has the richest Baroque pulpit in Norway. Much of the finance for the church came from Hanseatic merchants, which explains the large number of German inscriptions.

The oldest part of the **Cathedral** (Domkirken) dates from the late twelfth century while the choir and the lower part of the tower were built in thirteenth century Gothic style. It has extended over the centuries which accounts for the different styles.

Museums

Museums include **Bergen Fine Arts Museum**, Rasmus Meyers Allé, with alternating exhibitions of contemporary visual art; **Bryggens Museum** based on the extensive archaeological excavations of the Bryggen which took place between 1955 and 1972; the **Fishery Museum**; the **Hanseatic Museum** which is housed in one of the oldest and best preserved wooden buildings in Bergen; and the **Leprosy Museum**, home to the Bergen Collections of the History of Medicine. This is housed on the site of a hospital for lepers founded in the Middle Ages.

The **Museum of Cultural History**, Hårkon Sheteligs plass, 10, exhibits the culture and history of western Norway; the **Municipal Art Museum** has a collection of Norwegian paintings spanning 150 years; and the **Museum of Natural History**, Messeplass 3, includes the extinct Lofoten horse, a giant octopus and a number of whale skeletons.

PLACES OF INTEREST AROUND BERGEN

Old Bergen, Elesro, Sandviken, is an open-air museum with more than thirty-five wooden houses representing Bergen architecture from the early eighteenth century. The houses have been laid out in streets and the interiors have been faithfully restored to show what town life was like over three centuries ago. There are also period shops and a marketplace. It is situated north of Bergen, roughly where the tunnel bypass re-surfaces. Follow the road past the castle for a mile or so.

Hill Farm Museum, West Norway's Seter Museum, erected on Fanafjell, to the south of the city, shows what life was like on remote Norwegian summer farms over the centuries.

Langegaarden-Fjøsanger Hovedård, a marvellous manor farm with art gallery and handicraft shop, 10km from the city centre.

Ole Bull's Villa on the island of Lysøen, 19 miles/30km south of Bergen. It was designed by architect von der Lippe and built between 1872 and 1873 by the world-famous violin virtuoso and national hero Ole Bull. The villa contains

Three views of the waterfront (the Vågen).

Above: Rosenkrantz Tower.

Middle: A statue on the Bryggen.

Below: Part of the Bryggen, facing the waterfront.

his furniture and possessions at the time of his death in 1880 and the buildings are now protected as a national monument. Ole Bull built an 8 mile/13km network of paths all over the island and it is a delightful place to spend a few hours. The house is a mix of styles and is constructed from wood. He referred to his house as 'my little Alhambra'. Ole Bull was one of the greatest violin virtuosos of the nineteenth century and the inspiration for Edvard Grieg.

Damsgård Manor, Alléen 29, Laksevåg, about 2 miles/3km west of Bergen on Highway 582 was built around 1770 as Bergen's most splendid home and is now a museum. The garden, with its fountains and fishponds, has been restored to look as it did 200 years ago, showing the flowers, herbs, shrubs, vegetables and trees of that period. It is claimed that it is perhaps Europe's best preserved eighteenth century wooden building.

Alvøen Country Mansion is situated 7.5 miles/12 km west of Bergen and is the former 1797 residence of the owners, the Fasmer family. It was opened as a museum in 1983. It has a collection of furniture, porcelain, silver and textiles. There are guided tours on Sundays between noon and 4pm, May to September. **Troldhaugen,** Edvard Grieg's home for 22 years, was built in 1885 at Hop, a few miles to the south of the city. It is on a hill overlooking the peaceful Lake Nordås. The composer wrote many of his most famous works here and is buried here with his wife Nina. In the garden, with its

beautiful flowers and shrubs and twisty paths, there is the hut where he went to compose. A concert hall seating 200 has been built in the grounds and was opened in 1985.

Fantoft Stave Church was built in 1150 at Fortun in the Sognefjord area and moved to its present site at Fantoft in 1883. It was burnt down in June 1992 and has been carefully rebuilt in the original style.

Gamlehaugen, Gamlehaugveien 10, Fjøsanger, south of Bergen, is the official residence of the monarch when in Bergen. Not open whilst in residence, the house is otherwise open June – August but only 10am – 1pm. The gardens however are open throughout the year.

The **Fresco Hall**, Vagsalimen-ningen 1, now the **Tourist Inform-ation Office,** is opposite the quayside Fish Market and a real treat. It was built in 1862 as the Bergen Exchange. It has a wonderful arched ceiling and frescoes painted in 1920–21 showing working life in the country, such as fishing and shipbuilding. It is worth sitting down to take it all in once you have booked tours, obtained currency etc at the tourist office counter. ☎ 55 55 20 00; e-mail: booking @ visitBergen.com

The **Norwegian Arboretum** (open daily, admission free), Mildevågen was founded in 1971 and covers 50 hectares (125 acres), part of which is devoted to foreign trees and shrubs. The area has been beautifully land-scaped with hilly areas, gorges, a small lake and shoreline. ☎ 55 98 72 50

PLACES TO VISIT – IN AND AROUND BERGEN

Aquarium
Nordnesbakken, 4
☎ 55 55 71 71
Open: May-Aug, 9am-7pm; Sep-Apr,
10am-6pm.

Art Museum
Rasmus Meyers alle 3,7,9
☎55 56 80 00
Situated in three buildings by Lille
Lungegårdsvann Lake. Open: Daily
11am-5pm, 15 Sep-14 May closed
Mondays. Children free

Maritime Museum
Haakon Sheteligs plass, 15
☎ 55 54 96 00
Open: June-Aug, 11am-3pm; Sep-
May (except Sat) 11am-2pm.
Children and students free

Bergen Museum
Cultural History
H Sheteligs pass, 10
☎ 55 58 31 40

Natural History
Muséplass 3
☎ 55 58 29 20
Open: June-Aug, 10am-4pm (Sat &
Sun 11am, Monday closed);
Sep-May, Tues-Fri 10am-2pm; Sat-
Sun 11am-3pm; Monday closed
Children and students free, ticket
covers both museums on the same
day

Gamlehaugen
Gamlehaugen 10, Fjøsanger
☎ 55 92 51 20
The King's official residence in
Bergen area. Open: House June-1
Sep, Mon-Fri 10am-1pm. Gardens
open all year. House closed when
the King is in residence

Railway Museum
Garnes Station
☎ 55 24 91 00
Steam train on 11mile/18km line.
Take Hy16 via Indre Arna or train
to Arna and 5 minutes walk to old
Arna station. Departures: 5 June-11
Sep, Sundays 11.30am & 2.30pm
You can go by boat on the *MS
Bruvik* from the Bryggen and return
by bus. (Tickets from Tourist
Information office)

Troldhaugen
Hop (5 mile/8km south of Bergen)
☎ 55 92 29 92
Home of Edvard Grieg.
Open: May-Sep, 9am-6pm; Oct-Nov,
10am-2pm (Sat & Sun noon-4pm);
15 Jan-30 Apr, Mon-Fri 10am-2pm;
(Sat & Sun, noon-4pm).
Children free

Ole Bull's Villa
Lysøen Island
☎ 56 30 90 77
Open: 18 May-31 Aug, Mon-Sat
noon-4pm, Sun 11am-5pm; Sep,
Sun noon-4pm. Getting there:
contact Tourist Information Office
for car, bus or ferry options

Old Bergen Museum
Nyhavnsveien 4, 5042 Bergen
☎ 55 39 43 00
Open all year, free of charge but
charge for guided tour. Open air
museum with 40 buildings, guided
tours every hour and you need to
join one to gain access to the
houses.

If you are entering Norway by the ferry from England at Bergen, the road to Voss passes the dock gate. Remembering that in Norway you drive on the right, leave the quay and turn left. This road goes to Voss via Dale on the E16. Having settled down to driving in another land, the road is straightforward enough all the way to Dale, which is bypassed on a new road running along Bolstadfjord. The road is in a high-sided valley with many tunnels. Car parks with information boards at the roadside enable you to take a breather. Other than this, there is not much worth stopping for, but there are hints of things to come in terms of scenery.

Voss is a winter resort and much quieter in the summer, when its lake-side beach comes into its own. Soon after reaching the town you will pass the well-known Fleisher's Hotel on your left. Built in the late 1800s, it still draws the crowds. It sits on an elevated site, alongside the railway station and overlooking Vangsvatne, the adjacent lake with the beach. Opposite the hotel are motel-style units to let, which are run by the hotel. Virtually next door to the motel is the youth hostel if you prefer it.

The station is on the Oslo–Bergen railway line, one of the world's most scenic of lines and it deserves the reputation. If you are arriving in the country at Oslo, taking this railway to Bergen is a treat in itself. There is plenty of parking in the street in Voss, so park near the church with its broach spire (pay at the meters with a 'P' on the top). The Tourist Information Office, or *Sentrum* in Norwegian, is just to the right of the rear of the church, on the far side of the main road through the town. They can help with suggestions for all activities etc..

They have a Voss guide in English and various other languages. There is not much to seek out in the town. The church was built between 1271 and 77 and is open (free) in the summer. On the next block to the Tourist Information is the Post Office. Behind it is a house and behind that is Olav's Cross, erected in 1023 when the area converted to Christianity.

PLACES TO VISIT – VOSS

Voss Folkemuseum, The Molstertunet Museum
Tel: 56 51 15 11
voss.museum@2i.net
Situated on the hillside above Voss. The area map in the free Voss guide marks it – the road climbs out of town from near the church. Sixteen farm buildings from 1600 to 1870. Café.

Finnesloftet, Finnes Vegen
Tel: 56 51 16 75
Situated on the Bergen road (E16) about 1,000ft/300m beyond Fleischer's Hotel. Banqueting Hall dating from 1250. Norway's oldest secular building. Open only to groups, which is a pity.

Bordal Gorge
South of town, this deep and narrow gorge (only a few feet wide) has a footpath along it looking down onto the rushing white water.

NORTH FROM VOSS

From hereon in, you may assume that the scenery is wonderful virtually everywhere. Now and again your authors will use the occasional superlative, but most views are impressive and to keep saying so would be unnecessary repetition.

The E16 heads north out of town, After about 8mile/13km you reach the Tvinnefossen. It is a

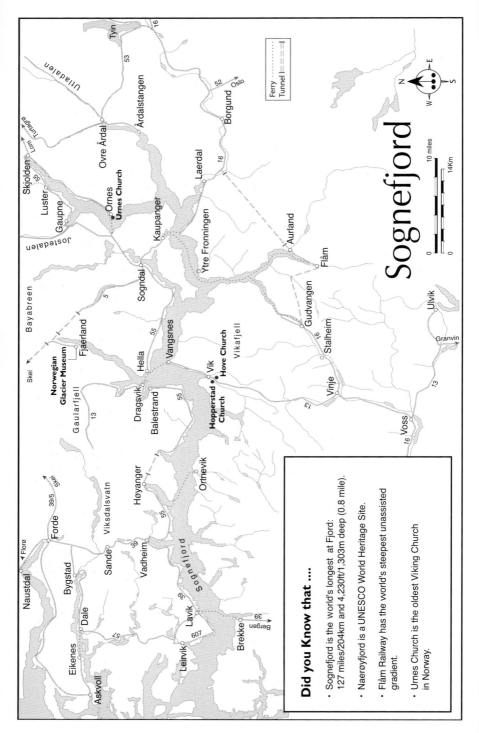

Sognefjord

Did you Know that ....

- Sognefjord is the world's longest at Fjord: 127 miles/204km and 4,230ft/1,303m deep (0.8 mile).

- Naerøyfjord is a UNESCO World Heritage Site.

- Flåm Railway has the world's steepest unassisted gradient.

- Urnes Church is the oldest Viking Church in Norway.

500ft/152m high waterfall. The E16 meanders through lovely scenery but with only limited opportunity to stop. You can stop by the waterfall (pull off the road to the left) and a few other places, such as rest areas or small car parks, some of which have a WC. At Vinje, highway 13 continues north, running over Vikafjell before dropping down to Vik and the Sognefjord. The E16 goes on through Oppheim to **Stalheim** at the top of **Naerøydalen**. Here is the Stalheim Gorge with magnificent views down the valley towards Gudvangen and the fjord. The road down the gorge was part of the King's Road between Oslo and Bergen, the initial post road. This still exists but has been replaced by an all-weather road incorporating several tunnels. This new road also takes out the many hairpin bends which featured on the earlier route.

Near to the Stalheim Hotel is a folk museum, which claims to be the most comprehensive privately owned museum in Norway. It has some 30 wooden buildings from the Voss area laid out as a traditional farm. If this is not impressive enough, an exhibition building houses over 5,000 exhibits. The attraction, Stalheim Folkemuseum, portrays Norwegian country life 150–200 years ago. Tel: 56 52 01 22, www.stalheim.com. The Stalheim Hotel has been serving visitors for generations and is a good place to call at.

The Naerøydalen is one of Norway's grandest and most popular valleys. There are two waterfalls at the gorge, the Stalheim and the Sivte, cascading down in grand style. It is a lovely drive down the valley to Gudvangen, covering several miles flanked by massive cliffs and several more impressive waterfalls. There is little at **Gudvangen** itself other than the ferry quay, hotels and the tourist buildings (the usual café, shops etc.).

Tourists have been taken down Naerøyfjord for about 150 years and the journey to Kaupanger is memorable for its scenery. It takes two hours, so there are not too many trips per day. Try and obtain the ferry times beforehand. Some stop in mid-fjord to exchange foot passengers for Aurland with another boat from Kaupanger. Passengers who need to change boat have to step from one ferry to the other in the middle of the fjord. The boats nudge up close together and lower ramps which overlap. Gudvangen is a popular ferry terminal and it pays to arrive in good time, especially in the midsummer months.

It is claimed that the fjord is the narrowest in the world. Because parts of Naerøyfjord are so narrow, mostly only 1,640ft/500m wide, and the mountains so high, towering almost 4,920ft/1,500m, the water is in shadow for many months of the year. During the summer, however, when the sun is at its highest, the water sparkles and stunning photographs can be taken. On a fine day the effect is breathtaking with lots of waterfalls crashing over the sheer rock faces. The fjord is claimed to be the narrowest in the world, being only 820ft/250m wide at its narrowest point. To the east Mount Stiganosi rises up to 5,776ft/1,761m and, in the waters below it, seals can often be watched at play. Cruise

The T-junction of Naerøyfjord and Aurlandsfjord with the flank of Mount Stiganosi on the right. It rises to 4,920ft/1,500m above sea (fjord) level.

Bakka on Naerøyfjord.

Kaupanger Stave Church.

ships still sail the fjord as far as Naerøyfjord, and it is an amazing sight to see a massive ocean liner lying anchored at the end of the fjord, dwarfed by the towering mountains.

Proceeding down Naerøyfjord and then Aurlandfjord, the Sognefjord is reached and then the ferry turns starboard (right) to head for Kaupanger. It soon passes the isolated village of Ytre Frønningen, on your right, which may be only reached by boat.

Upon reaching **Kaupanger**, take time to visit the Stave Church, built in 1184 and now restored to its former glory. It is outside the village, on the road to Sogndal and on your left, down a track. It is considered the best example of a stave church in Sogn. The Sognefjord Boat Museum (open daily Monday to Saturday) is also worth a visit, with a fine collection of boats dating from the nineteenth century. From highway 5 there is an exit to Sogndal airport at Hauksen. This road offers great views and there are a number of lookout points where you can pull in and take photos. The next stop is at the Sogn Folk Museum, famous for the Heiberg Collections – an open-air museum with indoor and outdoor exhibits dedicated to preserving the traditions of the region. It is open from dawn till dusk. A short journey on and you arrive at Sogndal, the commercial and service heart for the area, with its own university. It is a charming little town with many old houses and an interesting parish church.

Right: Kviknes Hotel, Balestrand.

PLACES TO VISIT IN THE SOGNDAL–KAUPANGER AREA

Kaupanger Stave Church
Open daily

Sogn Folk Museum / Fjord Museum (The Boat Museum)
6854 Kaupanger
Tel: 57 67 82 06
www.dhs.museum.no

ON TO BALESTRAND

Highway 55 to Helle runs close to the fjord. Look out for the 120m Kuinnafossen (waterfall) near Helle. Fruit trees abound along the way, in fact there are some 80,000 of them! Taking the ferry to Dragsvik, the town of Balestrand is just around the bay.

At **Balestrand,** take a walk along the quay. There are several old properties and a modern super-market. The former are worthy of a photograph, but the angle is tight to achieve anything worthwhile. There is a museum and a good art gallery here. Continue past these places to the front of the Kviknes Hotel. Now this place gives photo-graphers something to chew on. It is a resplendent wooden building recalling a past era when you would have not got anywhere near the place at times because of royal patronage. Its façade is a pure joy; completely over the top today but none the worse for that. Compare it with the modern addition at the rear (which regrettably dominates the area and skyline) and ask yourself which you prefer.

The Kaiser came here with presumably his countrymen in tow, but it is the British who are remem-bered. Like an outpost of Empire, they came for years, some staying and building in 1897 a mock stave church, St Olav's, close to the Kviknes Hotel. This Church of England outpost is part of the Diocese of Gibraltar; a waft of somebody else's former Empire in a land lorded over by Danes and Swedes before the Norwegians got it back just over a century ago.

Today, you can lord it like the Kaiser at the Kviknes Hotel, but ask specifically for a room in the grand old place, avoiding the new and brash-looking development at the rear and, more importantly, with a view over the lake. Alternatively, the youth hostel is behind the Kviknes, but a two-bedded room there was over 15Tel: more expensive than the nicely appointed NAF Camp cabins (*hyttes*) at Dragsvik, with views across the fjord to Balestrand.

The British established an art colony here and it has been a tourist resort ever since, but the Kaiser was not to be outdone. He erected in 1913 a huge bronze statue of the Viking King Bele in Balastrand and another of Bele's son-in-law, Fridtjov The Courageous, at Vangsnes! The latter is 72ft/22m in height. It is a pity he did not confine his use of bronze to artistic works instead of armaments. The year 1913 was the last year that the Kaiser came here. The following year he invaded Belgium and by treaty, Britain was a defender of Belgian neutrality.

BALESTRAND EXCURSIONS

1 THE GUDVANGEN– KAUPANGER FERRY

This has been discussed above (pp 57-59) on the basis that the trip out from Voss has been via this ferry. However, if Balestrand has been approached on highway 13 via Vangsnes, then an excursion to the ferry is recommended. It is suggested that you go via Vangsnes to Gudvangen. This is purely because once you reach Kaupanger, any available time can be used to visit the stave church, the Fjord or the Folk Museum. Public bus services are available and can incorporate excursions by both bus and ferry, but check timetables first.

Having taken the ferry to Vangsnes, the road hugs the fjordside to **Vik,** a small town which has seen much modern development. On the outskirts is Hopperstad stave church, just off the main road to the north (right). It was built in c. 1130 and is regarded as a classic example. A charge is made to visit the church, but a good photo is possible from the roadside.

Just beyond the turning to this church is a turning on the main road to the left to another ancient church – the Hove stone church (*steinkyrkje*). This is the oldest stone building in the Sogn area and was built in c. 1150. It makes a fascinating comparison and it is incredible that the two still survive.

The main road, highway 13, is soon climbing up to the lake-studded plateau of Vikafell at just under 3,250ft/1,000m above sea (fjord) level. The descent to Vinje, where the E16 is met, is a pleasant, mostly graded run, hugging a lake just before Vinje is reached (Hyrkdals Lake). At the junction with the E16, go left to Gudvangen.

2 JOSTEDALSBREEN GLACIER AND SOGNEFJELL

Taking highway 55 to Sogndal, the road turns north east for Gaupne, Luster and Jostedalen and climbs up onto Sognefjell and the Jotunheimen National Park (see below). Just 7.5 mile/12km from Sogndal turn right for **Solvorn**. The road drops steeply down to the attractive village with its traditional 'clapboard' cottages and its ferry to Ornes. Here is the Urnes (*sic*) stave church, renowned as being the oldest in Norway, dating from c. 1130. It incorporates intricate

carvings from an even earlier building. You can leave your car/bikes at Solvorn and go on foot to Ornes, or go with your transport to the head of the fjord, come down the far side and catch the ferry back to Solvorn. If you are wondering where the oldest Viking church is, it is not in Scandinavia, it is in England!

Solvorn car park is adjacent to the ferry and the Walaker Hotel: a good quality hotel; you can also take lunch etc. here. It consists of a collection of clapboard buildings with a newer, motel-style addition. It also has a well-known art gallery and has been in the same family for nine generations (since 1690). It enjoys superb views across the fjord.

From Solvorn, return to highway 55, which climbs up and over a mountain spur between two arms of the fjord. The highway twists along the edge of the turquoise-green fjord up to Skjolden. It is picturesque virtually the whole way and you can detour up Jostedalen to the Nigardsbreen Glacier from the village of **Gaupne**. For details on the glacier, see box on page 62. Highway 55 is narrow in places, especially towards the top end of the fjord, but it is not over-burdened with traffic. From **Skjolden**, continue down the other side of the fjord. If you propose to follow the itinerary to Andalsnes and Lom, the route brings you back to Skjolden and the opportunity to travel down the fjord to Urnes Church and the ferry to Solvorn.

Jostedalsbreen Glacier

The largest glacier on continental Europe (i.e. excluding Iceland) at 188sq mile/487 sq. km. It is one of the largest areas of wilderness remaining in southern Norway. Branches of the plateau glacier still stretch like fingers into the valleys. Two, Nigardsbreen and Boyabreen, are amongst the top tourist attractions in the country. The former is a Nature Reserve adjacent to the Jostedalsbreen National Park.

The area offers lots of hiking and the official Sognefjord guide leaflet describes a hike up to the Flatbreen cabin in Fjaerland, at 3,250ft /1,000 m above fjord level, as a once-in-a-lifetime experience. Icetroll at Jostedal offer mountain guides and kayaking in the Nigardsbreen area. **You are recommended not to go onto the ice without a guide.**

From Balestrand, the Bayabreen Glacier is much nearer, being above Fjaerland, with Flatbreen being just to the east of Bayabreen.

From the last week of June to the end of August, a bus leaves Sogndal for Nigardsbreen. Time is allowed for you to take a glacier hike before returning to Sogndal. On weekdays, this bus meets buses from Balestrand, Vik and Leikanger. Details from Tourist Information Offices.

You can approach the Nigard Glacier by boat. It speeds up your arrival and the water provides a great contrast to the ice on your photographs.

Contact: Brevegan AS–Brebaten Jostedalsrypa, Boks 294, 6852 Sogndal. Tel: 91 87 48 62 Post@brevegen.no ww.brevegen.no

CONTACTS

Norwegian Glacier Museum, Fjaerland
Tel: 57 69 32 88
Post@bre.museum.no
www.bre.museum.no

The Breheim Centre, Jostedalen
Tel: 57 68 32 50
Jostedal@jostedal.com
www.jostedal.com
Information office for the Jostedalsbreen National Park. You can book glacial hikes here.

Icetroll
Tel: 57 68 32 50
www.icetroll.com

Jostedalen Breførarlag
Tel: 57 68 31 11 / 57 68 32 50
www.bfl.no
Family hiking trips exploring the area and glacier.

Flatbreen Hiking Tours, Fjaerland Information Office
Tel: 57 69 32 33
www.fjaerland.org

Above: Nigardsbreen.

Sognefjell and the Jotunheim National Park

The highest mountain pass in northern Europe at 5,720ft/ 1,430m, it is a route for highway 55 running from Sogndal to Lom. From the top of the pass, you may detour by car from Galdesand to the Juvasshytta Lodge. At 6,100ft/1,850m, it is the highest point you can reach by car in Scandinavia. From the lodge you can continue on foot by guided tour to Galdhøpiggen at 8,147ft/2,469m, the highest mountain in northern Europe. In fact the Jotunheim has Norway's greatest concentration of peaks over 6,600ft/2,000m above fjord/sea level. At the summer ski resort at Galdhøpiggen, you can ski all year round and it is the only

summer resort in northern Europe offering super-G downhill skiing.

The road rises up from Skjolden, the most northerly point on Sognefjord (known locally here as Lusterfjord). The road was built in the Depression by 200 unemployed young men starting from here and also from above Lom. It replaced an old track and took two years to construct, largely without mechanical means, opening in 1938.

Close to the highest point is the Sognefjellshytta which offers food and accommodation. As you get above 1,000m, look for the height markers as you go through the next 100m mark up to 1,400m, crossing 1,430m at Fantesteinen, just on the Lom side of the Sognefjellshytta. The top of the pass is fairly flat and rugged. Look for the alpine flowers, but leave them for others to enjoy. This is a fragile, sensitive environment and needs treating and enjoying as such!

3 FLÅM, LAERDAL AND UTLADALEN

This route needs more decisions. It is suggested as a progressive route, but time/personal preference may be met by other options. These, however, involve some back-tracking. The area covered is south of the fjord. There is more spect-acular scenery, another stave church (aesthetically perhaps the best in the region) and the Flåm railway to get you high into the mountains.

From Balestrand or Hella, take the ferry to Vangnes and then highway 13 to Vinje.Turn left onto the E16 and proceed to Gudvangen, only this time ignore the ferry as you need to stay on the E16 to Flåm. This itinerary takes you on to Aurland, Laerdal, Borgund, Ardal, Turtagrø and back around to Sogndal and can be achieved by buses, which may be picked up in Gudvangen. However, the only ferry to Gudvangen is via Kaupanger.

The E16 from Gudvangen incorporates two long tunnels of 6.9 mile/11 km and 2.5 miles/4 km length before dropping down to **Flåm**. The village is full of souvenir shops and has little to keep you

THE FLÅM RAILWAY

Of the world's great railway journeys, the Flåm Railway justifiably sits amongst the best, yet it is one of the shortest. You may think the one hour or so journey is enough of a ride for one day anyway. So what are the details? It runs from Myrdal, where it connects with the Bergen–Oslo line, but not with a good road. It is 12.5 mile/20 km long and drops from 2,854ft/865m down to 6ft/2m above sea level at a maximum gradient of 1:18. It is claimed to be the steepest line worked by unaided locos anywhere in the world. The line has 20 tunnels and one bridge. One tunnel involves a complete loop as the line spirals to gain/lose height, depending on its direction.

Before you turn the page to read something else, it is worth knowing that it has five braking systems and any one of them will stop the electrified train. It is open all year round (but some of the trains may not run on Norwegian public holidays). It took 20 years to build and opened in 1940. It carries about 500,000 passengers a year. Despite the steep drop between the two terminal stations, the train travels slowly, even stopping at the most scenic spots.

Getting There

If you are travelling on foot from Balestrand to Flåm on the Express Ferry Boat, you can combine the railway trip with some very scenic walking, but you do have to keep an eye on the time. At the moment, this is the deal, but check the ferry and railway timetables for changes. You need to get the 8.30am boat out of Balestrand (mid-summer sailings). It reaches Flåm at 10.30am (the journey is not lacking in grandeur itself) and the train leaves at 11am (daily). You therefore need to get the 8.15am ExpressBoat from Balestrand which arrives at 10.40am (via Leikanger and Aurland). Tickets are available at the Tourist Information Centre. Trains on the line from Bergen & Voss stop at Myroal.

You get off at noon. Either return on the train or walk down the old constructors' road to Berekvam Station. This is recommended in the local guide as taking 2–2.5 hours. The train leaves Berekvam at 2.01pm, giving you two hours. The problem is that if you miss this and catch the next train, you get to Flåm only ten minutes the last ferry, it depends on you, but it is clearly worth checking out, especially if you are up to a brisk and clearly downhill walk.

Additionally, if you want to do this walk, you cannot use the Gudvangen–Flåm boat; the last return also having left before you get back. The best option is to use the bus or perhaps to walk as far as you like and stay overnight in Flåm. It takes about five hours to walk the whole way. You can hire a bike for the return, but some sections of the road are too steep to ride safely. For a timetable call 57632100, fax 57632350 or www.flamsbana.no

there other than the railway (see the feature box opposite for details). It is only 5 mile/8km to **Aurland**. Four mile/ 6.5km from Flåm is Otternes Farm. It consists of a former hamlet of 27 buildings, the oldest dating back to the seventeenth century. It is now used for folk activities, eg. spinning and weaving, baking and brewing. Open daily, 1 June – 15 September; Tel: 57 63 31 76, www.otternes.no

The old road from Aurland to **Laerdal** climbed to a height of 4,310ft/1,306m before dropping down Hodnadalen and covering 30 mile/48 km. Now it is much easier – although the old road is still available but usually closed between November and May. One of the longest road tunnels in the world now brings the two villages much closer. It is 15.3 mile/24.5 km long and opened in November 2000. It takes about 20 minutes to drive through and a special lighting system tries to physiologically divide the tunnel into four sections in the mind of the driver.

Laerdal is described in the official guide as having a 'dry and mild climate with possibilities for bicycling (*sic*), hiking and golfing almost all year round.' Worth remembering if you are elsewhere under dark skies. The old village hugging the fjord is the complete opposite to Flåm. Here, the heritage quarter consists of the whole village – 160 wooden properties built in the eighteenth century. Photographers eat your heart out and then move on to Borgund (see below).

There is a good assortment of craft workshops, art galleries, shops, etc. bringing new life to these buildings. Fortunately for the village, when other communities where rebuilding, Laerdal remained untouched. No doubt part of this was because of its (then) isolated situation. Now its importance is appreciated and the whole of the old quarter is preserved.

Worth going to see is the Norwegian Wild Salmon Centre/ Center on the bank of the river Laerdal. It opened in 1996 and glass panels enable you to see salmon, which have come back from the Atlantic to spawn. Some of the fish have not been caught and brought in – they arrived from the river via a fish ladder. Learn about the fish and fly-tying and watch a twenty-minute film on the life of the salmon as seen through the eyes of the fish.

Just short of 30 mile/48 km up the Laerdal valley is the stave church at Borgund. Although there are several in this area, they are in fact quite rare and this one is perhaps the best of the lot. Built in c. 1180, it is almost unaltered. In fact it has given its name to the Borgund style. It is also the most photogenic in the area. A new Stave Church Visitor complex opened in 2005 next to the church to highlight the significance of these Viking buildings. That they have survived at all is amazing, but virtually intact as is the case here is incredible.

From Borgund, the road continues up the valley to Borlaug, where it crosses the watershed, and on across Fillefjell, reaching a height of 3,343ft/1,013m. At Tyin on Lake Tyin, or rather just before

Above: The Flåm Railway at Høga, going down to Flåm. *(Morten Rakke/Visit Flåm)*

Below: The Laerdal Valley. *(Johan Berge/Innovation Norway)*

Above: The Norwegian Wild Salmon Centre, Laerdal.
(Pål Bugge/Innovation Norway)

Right: Borgund Stave Church.
(Johan Berge/Innovation Norway)

it, the E16 goes south-east, but this itinerary picks up highway 53 for Øvre Årdal, 30mile/50 km to the north-west. The road follows Lake Tyin for about 6 mile/9.5 km before heading up Tyedalen.

At **Øvre Årdal**, a narrow mountain road continues on for about 22 mile/35 km to the Turtagrø Hotel on highway 55, the road heading up to Sognefjell. However, before taking this – or heading back to Laerdal – another valley, **Utladalen**, beckons from Øvre Årdal. It is worth taking the road as far as the car park at Hjelle and walking from there up the road to Vetti and then taking the path to Vettifossen. The round trip takes about 2.5 hours. The waterfall is the highest in northern Europe, with a drop of just over 900ft/275m.

Utladalen is 25 mile/40km long and is surrounded by 50 peaks higher than 6,600ft/2,000m. Many hanging valleys, each with a waterfall, characterise the side walls of the main valley. It was designated a Landscape Preservation Area in 1980 and adjoins the Jotunheimen National Park to the north. If you can spend enough time here, guided walks are available. Contact Årdal Tourist Information for this and accommodation details.

The mountain road from Øvre Årdal to the Turtagrø Hotel is only open in the summer and is a toll road. The mountains on the west side are in the 1,400–1,500m bracket. Those to the east are higher with three above 6,600/2,000m at the northern end. A bus to Turtagrø leaves Øvre Årdal at 9.00am in summer months (confirm timetable with Årdal Tourist Information).

Both Øvre Årdal and Årdalstangan have an open-air swimming pool complex plus an indoor pool. Admission is free and the water is heated to a comfortable 25–28° C. From Turtagrø return to the Sognefjord at Skjolden on highway 55. The Turtagrø Hotel was built in 2002 following destruction by fire of its former, wooden predecessor. It makes a great place to be based for hiking in the adjacent Jotunheimen National Park.

4. FJAERLANDSFJORD BY BOAT TO THE GLACIER MUSEUM

Fjaerlandsfjord is 19 mile/30 km long. Much of it is quite isolated and the valley has only 300 inhabitants, yet 300,000 visitors call every summer! The magnet is the Jostedalsbreen Glacier, a plateau glacier with two branches which reach down towards Fjaerland – the Bøyabreen and the Supphellebreen Glaciers, the former being particularly scenic and the latter dropping down to 200ft/60m above fjord level. The glacier is easily seen from the road, or the flat roof of the Glacier Museum.

The Norwegian Glacier Museum is situated in **Fjaerland**. It tells you how glaciers form and have carved out the massive valleys around you to great depths, resulting in the fjords today. There is a lot to learn here and it is fascinating stuff. It is, however, a trip to the glacier which makes it all worth while and access is easy.

Visitors have been coming to the valley for over a century and the nearby Mundal Hotel dates from 1891. It is a massive wooden structure by the fjord. Mundal is described as being a 'book town', with a growing number of outlets and a reputation to match. However, it takes a bit of nerve to call the place a town.

One must not overlook Fjaerlandsfjord for its nature too. The head of the fjord is a nature reserve and some 90 different species of bird have been logged here. Out in the quiet waters of the fjord live the porpoise, although you can spot them in the main fjord too, their dorsal fins often giving away their presence. Once taken by fishermen, like the birds on the Fjaerland reserve, they are now protected.

Fjaerland may also be reached by road from Sogndal and also from Skei, both on highway 5.

Balestrand – Forde – Stryn

There are two routes on leaving Balestrand: north from town heading for Gaularfjell towards Skei or west down the fjord on highway 55. The latter is described here, although the former is equally scenic. For most of the way from Balestrand to Vadheim, the road hugs the fjord. It is the area where the fjord is at its deepest – 4,230ft/1,303m deep.

Nearing **Hoyanger**, the road disappears into a 4.4 mile/7km tunnel, emerging just outside the town. Hoyanger has a new central development incorporating both new and older properties. The latter includes a former house, now a museum of local industry. Look out for the various pieces of sculpture dotted about; some of them are rather accomplished.

There is a large aluminium works

here and although quite close to the middle of town, it appears unobtrusive when you are there. Between here and Vadheim there are good views of the fjord, but not too much to delay you once you get there. It has a few painted houses close to the waterside at the road junction of the E39 and the 55. Here is the car park if you wish to stop.

Forde is 25 mile/40km north from Vadheim via Sande. It is a reasonably sized town with most facilities. At the town crossroads, Skei is away to the right. However, if you are interested in seeing a small coastal town, continue on to Florø, some 44 mile/70km away via Naustdal on highway 5. The road has a toll on the west side of the Ramsdal Tunnel, a few miles out of Naustdal.

The latter possesses the best beach in the area, on the fjord and with the parish church as a backdrop at the edge of the beach. With its spire and painted walls, it is easy to locate. A short journey along highway 611 adjacent to Fordefjord brings you to Slettehaug Farm and the Luftkampmuseet. Open in the afternoons of June–August, it has a museum to commemorate an Allied airstrike on the German Navy in February 1945. It also has a café and farmers' market.

There is a new road into Florø on reaching Storebru. It passes the narrow passage of water between Eike and Solheimsfjords – the latter being nearest to the coast. The narrow gap is made worse by a long, narrow slip of land in mid-channel. If you have the time, a left turn at Eikefjord follows the fjord towards Stavang. At **Ausevik**,

Above: Solvorn.

Below: Urnes stave church. *(Per Eide/Innovation Norway)*

Above: Strynfjord.

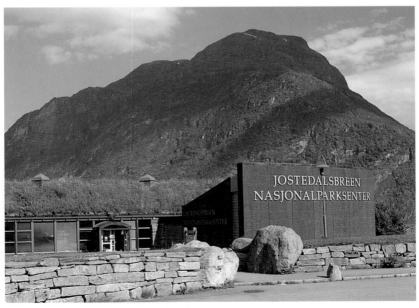

Above: Jostedalsbreen National Park Centre, Oppstryn.

beneath Skålefjell, are over 300 rock carvings, which are over 3,000 years old.

The carvings feature humans, animals and various other symbols carved on exposed slabs of rock. Virtually due north of this site is another, much larger site at Vingen. This is off the Svelgen–Isane ferry road (highway 614). Here there are 2,500 figures and it is claimed that they date from an impressive 8,000 years ago.

Florø is a fishing town and many people come here for the fishing or diving. The Krokane Camp on the approach to town has cabins for hire, sleeping from two to eight persons. It has facilities for fishermen, with an area for gutting, freezing or smoking. There is a changing room for divers, but no compression chamber (there is one in Florø). The camp is on the coast road signposted to Solheim on leaving town. It has a beach too.

On the third weekend in June, Florø hoists the world's largest Herring Table. It is put up in the street and is 1,300ft/400m in length! The table is loaded with herring dishes served with bread, potatoes and drinks. Even better, it is all free! For other times of year, the Kake–Bua quayside café and coffee house may be of interest. It is situated in a 160-year old restored warehouse and has exhibits relating to the fishing industry.

Florø is sheltered by a range of islands, several of which are linked by ferry. If time permits you might like to consider a trip to one or more of them. Kinn, for instance, has a church dating back to the twelfth century. Once the home of many people in the fishing industry, Kinn now has just eleven inhabitants. There are more details in the Florø area guide to island visits.

Finally, if your interest covers old watermills, then just about 12 mile/ 20km out of Florø, as you return to Forde, to the left is the road to Svelgen (highway 614). It crosses the fjord and then heads west for a short while before turning north. Ahead is Terdal, where a series of mills have been renovated. They date from the eighteenth century and have four waterwheels. Opening times from the Tourist Information in Florø.

Forde to Stryn

Forde is a new town extending to its current size from a small farming village in the last thirty years or so. It has developed into the most important business community between Bergen and Ålesund to the north. It hosts an annual international folk music festival every July. It is now the biggest in Norway (www. fordefestival.no). The town makes a good base for exploring the area.

Between Forde and Moskog is the Sunnfjord Museum. It is an open-air museum with a collection of timber houses dating back to the 17th-Century. It also has a herb garden, coffee shop and a trail to the Huldefossen Waterfall. (Open: June–August, Mon–Fri, 10am–6pm; Sat–Sun noon–5pm. Shuts Mon-Fri, 4pm in June and last 2 weeks in August. Rest of the year open in the week 10am–3pm by advance booking. Tel: 57 72 12 20.

At **Vassenden**, you reach Jolstravatnet. Look out for the

wooden-built Jolster Hotel on your left and on a bend in the road plus the Jolstra Museet (Jolstra Museum). This is a privately owned museum consisting of thirteen houses and a huge collection of domestic items arranged in the rooms of the houses. It is only open mid-May to mid-August and only at weekends from noon–5pm, with-out booking in advance. Tel: 57 72 73 71; www.jolstramuseet.no)

The Tourist Information Offices at Forde and Skei can give you details on fishing, guided walks and whitewater rafting.

Much of the E39 towards Stryn from Forde runs along Jostravatnet in the county of Sogn og Fjordane. Extending to an area of 260 sq. miles/671 sq. km, the country has 35 sq. miles/90 sq. km of glaciers and 16 sq. miles/43 sq. km of water. The journey alongside the lake's broad expanse is pleasant, although the mountains are lower than those hugging Sognefjord or to the north. The lake is renowned for its trout.

At **Skei**, highway 5 heads to the south-east, disappearing into a tunnel under the southern tip of the Jostedalsbreen Glacier. It emerges a few miles from Fjaerland and the Glacier Museum. If you go beyond Fjaerland, there is a toll station just out of the village.

The E39 heads north at Skei along the Våte Valley, passing the Nons Waterfall near Egge and a lake on your left. Look out for the goats, which frequent this road high in the mountains. At **Byrkjelo**, take highway 60 to the right for Utvik, where the Innvikfjord branch of the Nordfjord is reached. Despite the latter in general being

a beautiful stretch of water, the length between Utvik and Olden could frankly be better. At Olden, a minor road runs south to Briksdal and its glacier, an arm of the Jostedal glacier. Another road at Loen does similar, heading for Kjenndal, and is shorter. **Loen** has a grassed area opposite the large Hotel Alexandra. Here you can park, picnic, stroll or just admire the fjord before heading for Stryn or the glacier. Loen is the most easterly point on Nordfjord; as the crow flies it is about 65 mile/ 100km from the sea.

Stryn Excursion

Ten and a half mile/17km south of Loen at the end of the Lodal valley is the **Kjenndalen valley** and just a fifteen-minute walk to the glacier. Despite the global reduction in the size of glaciers, this one actually grew about 1,000ft/300m between 1980–97, but appears to be in retreat once more. The Kjendalen valley is one of the wildest in western Norway. If you wish to walk on the glacier however, contact Olden Tourist Information; Tel: 47 57 87 3126 never walk on the glacier without a professional guide.

As an alternative, you can catch the boat down Loenvatnet, the lake running down the valley from the Hotel Alexandra at Leon. The departure is at 10.30am, returning at 1.15pm. The boat takes you down to Kjenndalssanden and a coach then takes you to the glacier. This is a daily service between 1 June and 1 September. The timing of departure may change because of pre-booked tours, so it is worth

Above: Geirangerfjord. *(Per Eide/Innovation Norway)*

Above: The ferry from Stranda at Gravaneset.

Opposite page: The view towards Stryn from the top of Hjelledalen.

ringing ahead on Tel: 47 57 87 50 50. Children under 10 go free.

In 1905 and again in 1936, massive amounts of rock slipped off Mt Ravnefjell, causing a tidal wave in the lake below (Loenvatnet). The villages of Nesdal and Bødal were inundated and a total of 135 people died. There is a memorial to them at Loen church.

From Olden, you can reach the **Briksdal Glacier** at the end of the Oldedal Valley. From the car park there is a short walk to the glacier, or you can travel by open car. One of the most used scenic photographs of Norway is of a pony and trap on the bridge at Briksdal with the glacier behind, so the area may be familiar to you prior to your arrival. It also means that you are likely to have the benefit or otherwise of a lot of company.

From Loen, it is a short distance to **Stryn**, the regional town for shopping and commerce. With its wide main street and shops, you could be forgiven for thinking that this is a new town like Forde, but you would be wrong. A clue is passed on a right-hand bend in the road just before you reach town. Here are two old wooden buildings, both hotels. The left-hand one dates from 1850 and the other – a more interesting building to look at, in Swiss-Dragon style – dates from 1898. The former is the Visnes Hotel and the latter is now the Villa Visnes (but formerly the King Oscar's Hall Hotel, having been lovingly restored by its former owners, a Norwegian and American couple). The hotels are now run by the fifth and sixth generation of the Visnes family, offering high quality food and comfort. It is easy to miss them from the road. The drive is some distance from the bend, but it is worth the detour to see them.

Stryn has been receiving tourists since the English arrived in the 1860s to fish for salmon. There are many attractions, from a trip to the glacier; a boat trip on the fjord; the Jostedalsbreen National Park Centre/Center at Oppstryn on Strynsvatnet; and further along the same road (highway 15), the National Tourist Road – Gamle Strynefjellsvegen – highway 258, branches away for Grotli. This ancient highway passes the summer ski school (Tel: 47 57 87 54 74) and picnic areas and is very scenic. A bonus is to complete a circular route by returning on highway 15. Get ready to stop on leaving the last tunnel. If the sun is out, the view to Strynsvatnet down to Hjelledalen is alone worth the trip.

Before leaving Stryn, if time permits, it is worth taking a detour. Take highway 15 westwards out of town to explore the north side of the Nordfjord. After about 4 mile/ 6 km, take highway 613 to the left. It follows the fjord to Hopland and Randabygd, a distance of 13.75 mile/ 22km. There are terrific views of the fjord, from sea level up to a height of over 1,625 ft/500m. There is a beach at Hopland if the weather permits.

Stryn – Geiranger – Stranda – Andalsnes – Lom

Leaving Stryn on highway 15, the road to Geiranger runs along a flat, cultivated valley towards Strynsvatnet (Lake Stryn) and the village of Oppstryn. Here, both the church and the National Park Office are to be found between the road and the lake. The Nasjonal Park Senter has lots of information on the Jostalsbreen National Park. However, you cannot get into even the shop without paying the admission fee. There is a picnic area here with a backdrop of the mountains to which the road leads you.

Beyond Strynsvatnet, the road begins to climb, reaching 1,950ft/600m at the junction of highway 15 and highway 258. You have a choice of either road to reach Langevatnet and highway 63, the road to Geiranger. This road junction is at a height of 3,016ft/928m. It rises even higher to 3,373ft/1,038m at the side of a lake – Djupvatnet. This has accommodation at the far end of the lake, at the Djupvasshytta, which also offers food if you are just passing. The lake is overlooked on both sides by high mountains and the area is decidedly alpine. Opposite the hotel a road climbs up towards the summit of Dalsnibba, which reaches a height of 4,890ft/1,495m.

There is a toll to pay, but the 3 mile/5km road to the top repays with fantastic views across the area and down to **Geirangerfjord**. As an alternative to taking your own vehicle to the top, a bus leaves Geiranger in the morning and another leaves in the afternoon. Details from the Tourist Information Office, or www.fjordl.no. After crossing Blåfjell, highway 63 begins its descent to Geiranger.

The view to Geiranger from the mountain behind the town must be one of the most well-known countryside views in the world. Often taken with cruise ships anchored just off the end of the fjord, the scene portrays the near vertical cliffs, which drop huge distances to the water. It is a breathtaking view and Geiranger is often claimed to be the most beautiful of all of Norway's many fjords. Quite often the view is taken from a rock overhang, with the photograph incorporating someone sitting on the very edge of a huge drop. It's either a clever use of graphics or someone being reckless, so don't even think of trying to emulate it.

The town has been spoilt, not surprisingly, with a desire to cash-in on the tourists, many coming ashore from the cruise ships to take a few snaps and shop. If 'kiss me quick' hats are not for sale here, it's a wonder. In an attempt to redress some of this, the Norsk Fjordsenter (Tel: 70 26 38 010) has been built. Its theme is the life and activities of the fjord's people, portraying the heritage of the area. Authentically recreated buildings and their furnishings create a good impression of what life was like.

The best way of discovering the fjord is on the ferry to Hellesylt. The precipitous sides to the fjord preclude any possibility of a road or track. A recording in English highlights the various features enroute. From July to the end of September, it is unusual not to find at least one cruise ship here, with about 150 calling during this period (nearly half being German and a quarter being British and including the *QE II* and the *Queen Mary II*). This excludes the daily Hurtigruta express coastal steamer. Even if it's an overcast day, these large ships enable you to enhance your photographs back towards the town and its huge backcloth of mountain scenery. Remember that the ships are 70mile/112km from the coast.

The ferry criss-crosses the fjord, highlighting not only why this is the best fjord in Europe, let alone Norway, but also picking out waterfalls and isolated farmhouses (now refurbished and restored by a trust after being abandoned). Some were only accessed by ladders; even children helped with the harvest, tied to a rope on dangerously precipitate slopes. Perhaps the best story is about the farmer who pulled up the cliff ladder to prevent the taxman getting to him!

From mid-April to mid-September, there is a fast ship service to the area from Bergen. It leaves

Tresfjord Church, dwarfed by adjacent cliffs.

there at 8pm, arriving at Ålesund in the morning and reaching Geiranger at lunchtime. You really need to stay over, for the return journey (on a different vessel) is only 15 minutes after arrival. Up-to-date details are available from Tourist Offices. There is also a car ferry from Geiranger to Valldal (one at lunch-time and another early in the evening between mid-June and mid-August. It takes 2.25 hours).

The most spectacular feature of Geirangerfjord has to be the Seven Sisters Waterfall on your right. Opposite is another one, known as The Suitor and further on, before Geirangerfjord meets Sunnylvsfjord, is the Bride's Veil Waterfall, again on the right, so maybe The Suitor 'got lucky'. Let's hope so! If the waterfalls are spectacular, then the whole fjord clearly is something grander and certainly memorable. In places, the rock faces are vertical as they plummet into the deep waters of the fjord. Some of these bear the names of cruise ships which have been here.

At the T-junction with Sunnylvsfjord, the ferry bears left for Hellesylt. As you dock, ahead is the best view of the village's waterfall, Hellesyltfossen. Above and to the right sits the youth hostel with a line of a dozen cabins to the left of the painted building. The trip takes 65 minutes from Geiranger. The youth hostel is only open in the summer and the views are terrific. In the quiet of early morning, as the sun reaches the fjord and the early Geiranger ferry turns the bend into the waters near Hellesylt, you face yet another scene to savour and remember. The cabins

Mount Blåtind from near Vågstranda on Romsdalfjord.

The valley to Berill from near Innfjorden.

Lom Stave Church, built by the Vikings.

are inexpensive and there is a good atmosphere in the main building. Water for the cabins has to be fetched from the main building.

Finally, Geirangerfjord is also served by a sightseeing boat, which sails around the fjord and returns to Geiranger between mid-May and mid-September. It leaves the Old Quay by the Tourist Information Office. The service takes 1.5 hours but is not that frequent, so check times beforehand if you can.

In the village of **Hellesylt** is the Peer Gynt Gallery, which also has a café. It exhibits carvings in wood by Oddvin Parr based on scenes from Ibsen's famous *Peer Gynt* (Tel: 70 26 38 80). The Grand Hotel here dates from 1871 and is one of the oldest fjord hotels on the west coast (Tel: 70 26 51 00).

From Hellesylt, highway 60 climbs up above the fjord with excellent views other than when you are in a series of three tunnels. The road leads to the head of Strandadalen and drops gradually down this attractive valley to Stranda and the ferry to Gravanes. Stranda is a small community with a wide variety of shops, should you need them. The ferry takes fifteen minutes only and the timetable states Stranda–Liabygda, which is misleading, as the quay is well out of town, at Gravanes.

The ferry affords views of both Storfjord to the left, which leads to the sea, and on the right to two branches – Sunnylvsfjord, behind you, which leads to Geirangerfjord, and ahead, Norddalsfjord, leading to Valldal. Upon reaching the shore, the road quickly climbs up to a tunnel. Upon returning to daylight, bear left at a junction on highway 650 to **Stordal**. Just before reaching town having come down the valley with the same name, look out for the Rose Kyrkja (Rose Church) on the right. It dates from 1797. A tall stone outside the churchyard and at the roadside marks the struggle for Norwegian independence in the early nineteenth century. Note also the collection of old buildings to the right of the church.

From the town of Stordal, the road keeps close to Storfjord and turns inland on the jointly numbered E39/E136 having reached Sjøholt. The road climbs up to Ørskogfjell at 1,100ft/338m, before descending Skorgedalen to **Tresfjord**. Continue on E136 to the village of the same name (Tresfjord). The church has an isolated site with a magnificent mountain backdrop. Here a minor road goes to Ovstedal, dominated by some of the many mountains in the range of 4,390ft – 4,875ft/ 1,350–1,500m. The distinctive, white painted church dates from 1825. From here, there is a pleasant run close to the fjord on the road to Vestnes and Romsdalfjord, which is followed to Andalsnes, with lovely scenery all the way.

Frankly, there is little to keep you in **Andalsnes**; it is a modern community with memories of the railway station and industrial estates. From here, the itinerary follows highway 63 along Isterdalen heading for Trollstigen, which means Troll's Ladder; it sums up the road rather nicely. The gradually rising road heads for a wall of rock, the road switch backing up to the top. With bends which are almost vertically in line with the next but one above, the road is either an adrenaline rush or a hair-raising experience. It passes the Stigfossen waterfall, which drops 650ft/200m. It is close enough to the road to cover it and your vehicle with spray. A car park at the top of the climb gives you the opportunity to take the necessary photographs of the view back to Isterdalen and to stop for a break.

From here, the road continues up Langdalen before descending to Valldall and the ferry from Linge to **Eidsdal** across Norddalsfjord. Valldall boasts rafting on one of Norway's best rafting rivers. If you feel up to it, telephone Valldall Naturopplevingar on Tel: 90 01 40 35. If you fancy a quiet road and a run down the fjord, go left in **Valldall** down Tafjord. Do not be put off by the power station or the lack of old houses by the fjord-side at Tafjord village. They were swept away by a tidal wave in 1934 as a result of a huge avalanche.

From Eidsdal, highway 63 climbs from sea level up to 2,028ft/624m before descending to Geiranger-fjord and a scenic run into the village of Geiranger. From here, retrace steps up the mountainside to reach Djupvatnet (Lake Djup) and its alpine scenery and plants. Just beyond the lake is a T-junction between highway 63 and highway 15. To the right, the entrance to the top tunnel on the road to Stryn is ignored, for our route goes ahead alongside Breidalsvatnet to Grotli and the top of the old road from Stryn (now highway 258).

The alpine scenery soon gives way to the descent into Ottadalen. Passing through Bismo, Lake Otta is soon reached with highway 15 running down the south side into **Lom**. Buses seem to run in and out of Lom all day long. It is an important tourist venue with the main focus being on its wooden stave church, now 1,000 years old. Sounding quite recent in comparison is the Lom Open Air Museum. It includes 23 listed houses dating from 1600 to 1900. It is open from mid-June to the end of August, from 11am to late in the afternoon (times vary). Adjacent to the stave church is Loarutsalg, which sells local handicrafts and craft art. It is open mid-June to mid-August, 9am–8pm. There are many shops in Lom, catering for most requirements.

The Tourist Information Office is open for most of the year, but times vary. Lom is a good tourist destination with a lot of activities available in the area.

From Lom, highway 55 leads to the Jotunheimen (see page 63). It is a scenic route, which improves with height until you reach the top. See also the choice of routes into Sognefjord, either down highway 55 or down to Urnes stave church from Skjolden and then taking the ferry to reach Solvorn and then highway 55 again (see page 61).

Left: Boats at Granvin

Below: Sørfjord, a branch of Hardangerfjord, at Lofthus.
(Per Eide/Innovation Norway)

Hardanger stretches 112miles/179km from the sea. Like the Sognefjord, it has some fantastic scenery and is well worth including in your itinerary. One of the most scenic branches is at the eastern end – Sørfjord. It is 25miles/40km in length but not very wide. Travelling down the east side affords the most spectacular of its views – across the fjord and up to its peaks rising above 4,875ft/1,500m and, at the southern end, up to the Folgefonno Glacier. Here the ice-covered mountains can be clearly seen, offering summer skiing opportunities.

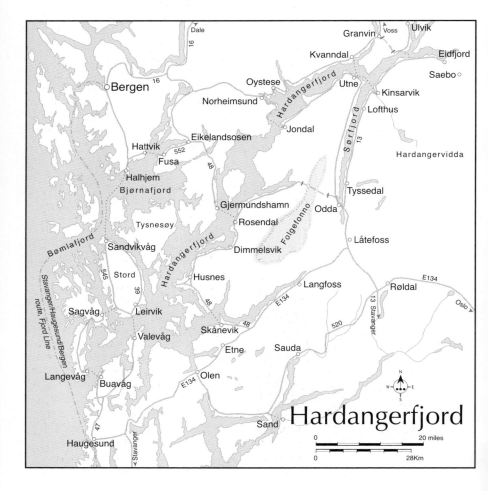

The Sørfjord has been catering for the needs of visitors for centuries. The Utne Hotel, for instance, has been opening its doors continuously since 1722. Kaiser Bill came to the area (but left no bronze statues of the Vikings) and visitors have shared its delights with Norwegian royalty, the rich and the famous from around the world. Perhaps one of its most endearing guests was Edvard Grieg. He came in 1877 with his wife Nina and stayed at the Hotel Ullensvang at Lofthus. He had a little wooden cabin constructed in an isolated spot looking down on the fjord. Here he composed some of his finest pieces including *Peer Gynt*. The hotel is still there and so is the cabin; at least it is down in the hotel grounds now, but it can still be seen.

Today the area has several musical festivals. The Hardanger Music Festival is held at Ullensvang in mid-May. Norheimsund hosts in June the Hardingtonar, a series of concerts and various other events including the Boat Festival. Odda

Greig's cabin in which he composed *Peer Gynt*, Hotel Ullensvang, Lofthus.

has a Blues weekend in mid-June and at the end of September or early October. A couple of churches have organ recitals: Jondal and the ancient stave church at Roldal in the south of the area. These are a weekly event during July. See **www.hardangerfjord.com** for 'What's On' and more up-to-date information on times.

There is a whole host of other activities available to keep you occupied in this area. There are all sorts of sightseeing tours, fjord cruises, hiking trips, glacier walks, kayak cruising, summer skiing at the Folgefonno Summerski Centre, etc. These are all listed on the area web site or in the annual Hardanger-fjord tourist leaflet. Just look for the one with the British flag or you may walk out with one in a foreign language.

In addition to activity-based attractions, there are six museums in the area: the Folk Museum at Utne; the boat building museum at Norheimsund; the 'cluster yard' of buildings with one dating from AD 1250 at Agatunet (☎ 53 66 21 14), which is virtually opposite Lofthus on the other side of the fjord. Others are the work of Ingebrigt Vik, one of Norway's finest sculptors, at Øystese, near Norheimsund; the Kvam Bygde museum where the painter Adolph Tideman worked and the Holvenstova, an eighteenth century house in the Bygdetunet (village square) at Granvin. Just outside Norheimsund (to the west) is Steinsdalsfossen. You can walk around the back of the waterfall having left your vehicle in the nearby carpark, just off Highway 7. The latter is a national scenic road

Lapp Store, Highway 13 above Granvin on the road from Voss.

Early morning tranquility at Lake Granvin.

The quay at Granvin.

Kinsarvik (by the ferry terminal).

Kinsarvik Church, which dates from c. 1160AD.

in the Hardangerfjord area.

Hardanger is the fruit garden of Norway. The area has some 600,000 fruit trees with 512,000 of them in Sørfjord. The cherry and plum blossom is at its best in early May, with the apple blossom following on in late May. The Ullensvang area grows 80 per cent of Norway's cherry crop and about thirty different species of apple are grown. In season (August), you can buy the fruit from many stalls at the roadside. Some are manned but others rely on an honesty box.

The fruit trees were first planted by monks at Lofthus in AD1200–1210. A grange of the Cistercian monastery in Bergen (run by English monks) was established on the site of Opedal farm in Lofthus. The only reminder of their activity here is the fruit industry and a route up onto the Hardangervidda Plateau. It incorporated 616 stone steps, now known as the Monk's Steps (Munketrappene).

The Hardangervidda is now a National Park and is the largest in Norway. It is also northern Europe's largest mountain plateau. It may be explored using waymarked paths which connect various lodges. It is a wild, unspoilt area, where reindeer, moose, roe and red deer roam. You may be lucky and spot wolverine, pine martin and lynx, the golden eagle and buzzard. Eidfjord in the north is a good starting point to explore the plateau. South of the town are the valleys of Hjølmodalen and Måbodalen which are orientated at 90 degrees to each other at Ovre Eidfjord. The road up Hjølmodalen heads for Vivelid and the Valurfossen. This major water-fall has a fall of 591ft/182m and there is a path to the foot of it. It takes 90 minutes to get there and back from your vehicle or bike, which should be left near the uppermost opening of the Måbø tunnel in Måbødalen.

There is the Hardangervidda Nature Centre/Center in Eidfjord. It covers biology, botany, glaciation and ornithology. It has a tourist information desk, shop and restaurant.

If you want to learn more about exploring the Hardangervidda, contact the Bergen Mountain Hiking Association (www.bergen–turlag.no). They publish a book, *Norwegian Mountains on Foot,* and a helpful leaflet, which gives information on what to expect and also details of the lodges. Their address is Bergen Turlag, Tverrgaten 4–6, 5017 Bergen, ☎ 55 33 58 10, e-mail: post@bergen–turlag.no.

HARDANGERFJORD ITINERARY

This itinerary follows on from an excursion around the Sognefjord area and therefore approaches the Hardangerfjord from the north. It can easily be approached directly from Bergen or Stavanger, although the latter includes a stretch of much lower, less interesting scenery and several additional ferries, especially if one is heading north towards Bergen first.

Heading south from the Sogne region, you need to make for Voss. From there, highway 13 heads for Granvin (in fact you bypass Voss, in case you need to go into town). The road climbs up into the mountains and then descends past a Lapp (Sami) store selling mementos at the side of the road. The road drops quickly to Lake Granvin, which is reached just after the Hardanger region sign. There is a campsite with cabins (*hytte*) just across the road from the lake shore. There is an attendant until mid-evening if you are needing somewhere to stay.

Granvin is a small place with a pleasant quay area at the head of a branch of the fjord (Granvinfjord) with a logging complex nearby. You take a right turn to reach it just before the Vallavik tunnel on the road to Bruravik and its ferry to Brimnes. As mentioned above, Granvin has some venerable buildings, one of which is open as an attraction, but there is not a great deal of interest here to delay you for too long.

There is even less to delay you at Bruravik other than the ferry, for there is no community here. The nearest village is Utvik, 6 miles/10 km further along Osafjord. Having caught the ferry, highway 13 continues from Brimnes down the east side of Sørfjord to Odda. While on the ferry, there are views up Osafjord to Vassfjøro, which rises to 5,307 ft/1,633m, as well as westwards towards Utne and the mountains beyond. The view extends towards Samlen, which rises to 2,230ft/683m.

From Brimnes, the road to Kinsarvik hugs the side of the fjord with memorable views across the water. **Kinsarvik** is only a small village with the ferry to Kvanndal via Utne, very useful if you are having a short detour to the fjord from Voss. There is a car park adjacent to a supermarket and a Tourist Information Office virtually opposite the turning to the ferry quay. It is worth stopping here for a few minutes – the village is tucked between high mountains and the water's edge. The church is one of the oldest stone churches in Norway, dating from c. AD1160. It is situated at the side of the road, opposite the car park and supermarket.

Behind Kinsarvik is Husedalen, a valley which cuts into the Hardangervidda. The valley has four large waterfalls. The first to be reached, after 2.5 miles/4km, is the smallest (always the way if you are in a hurry). It is Tveitafossen, with the other three extending the walk to three hours. From Lofthus, there is another trail, this time along the River Opo, which leads to the Opofossen, Norway's third largest waterfall with a drop of 2,112ft/650m in total. Beyond it is another waterfall, Skrikjo, which has a drop of some 1,300ft/400m. This trail takes about two hours.

A short distance beyond Kinsarvik is **Lofthus**. It is situated opposite mountains, which stretch along the west side of the fjord to the Folgefonno glacier. Virtually opposite Lofthus is Aganut, which reaches a height of 4,904ft/1,509m. Lofthus is the home of the region's folk museum and Hotel Ullensvang, one of the finest hotels in Norway. It has been rebuilt several times but it is still owned by the descendants of its founder, whose first guests arrived in 1846.

Guests have included Edvard Grieg, whose cabin may still be seen here. It was originally built on

Hotel Ullensvang, Lofthus.

Sørfjord from Hotel Ullensvang, Lofthus.

Above: Bronze of horse, Odda

Above and below: Låtefoss on the road to Roldal from Odda.

the hillside above so that the composer could do his work in peace and quiet and for the most part uninterrupted. It eventually turned up on Bokn Island, between Stavanger and Haugesund. About to be used for keeping hens, it was rescued and re-erected adjacent to the fjord, in the grounds of the hotel where the composer and his wife Nina had stayed for long periods.

It was just large enough for a piano, table and chair. Grieg had a small summer house in his garden at Troldhaugen, near Bergen, where he also composed some of his pieces. When listening to his work it is pleasant to think of the great man making his compositions within the simplicity of two little wooden buildings close to the serenity of an adjacent fjord. It is hard to think that he did not draw inspiration in this way. The hotel has a leaflet on its development, the Utne family who still own it and their connection with the illustrious composer. In an expensive country, the cost of staying in such magnificent surroundings seems relatively inexpensive, especially out of season.

Upon reaching Lofthus, decisions need to be made having regard to the amount of time available. If it is pressing, a return to Kinsarvik enables you to take the fery to Kvanndal and then take highway 7 to Nordheimsund and on towards Bergen. An alternative route is to go on to the end of Sørfjord to Odda. **Odda** is largely a new-looking town with not a lot to delay you. A one-horse town springs to mind, but one must not be unfair; there is a large bronze of a horse between the car park and the waterfront!

Continuing south, this route enables you to stop and admire the Låtefoss – waterfall – (along with a crowd of others) before swinging south-west on highway E134 for Haugesund. Highway 13 continues its journey south, and then south-west to Stavanger. Off this route is the road to Roldal and its stave church, which hosts the music festival (see above).

The river at Låtefoss splits into two, creating two waterfalls adjacent to each other, falling to the road-side. The height isn't great but the volume of white water falling amidst a cloud of spray does have some sense of the dramatic.

It time permits, you can pass through Odda to the far side of Sørfjord and onto highway 550. Take highway 48 through the Folgefonn Tunnel (there is a toll) and continue down Mauranger-fjord, a branch of Hardangerfjord west of the Folgafonno ice-sheet, to Rosendal. Just south of here, near to Seimsfoss, is Baroniet Rosendal. This is the only barony in Norway, being the creation of the King of Denmark. The house was built in 1665 by Ludwig Rosenkranz and gifted to the University of Oslo in 1927, having been in the Rosenkrone (*sic*) family since 1745. The buildings are a mixture of Baroque and Renaissance. There is an annual music festival held each May. The Barony Play is also performed here each July. The park is open to the public daily but house opening times vary so check with the local tourist office.

The house has been preserved as

it was when the last owners left it. Its china, paintings and furniture are of interest. The house is set in parkland with a large and lovely rose garden. The old building sits at the foot of the mountains, the hundreds of roses making a lovely foreground. There is a tea room here, with the opportunity of sitting outside if the weather permits. Just to the north of the town is Kvinnherad church, built in Gothic style and dating from the Middle Ages.

From here, return to Løfallstrand (just north of Rosendal) for the ferry to Gjermundshamn and highway 48 towards Bergen. Upon reaching Eikelandsosen, bear left on highway 552 to Fusa and then take the ferry to Hattvik. Proceed to Osøyro and take the E39 into Bergen.

HARDANGER TOURIST OFFICES

Eidfjord
5783 Eidfjord
☎ 53 67 34 00
www.eidfjordinfo.com

Granvin
Postboks 8, 5733 Granvin
☎ 56 52 53 60/56 52 40 00
www.granvin.kommune.no

Jondal
5627 Jondal
☎ 53 66 85 31
e-mail:
jondal.tourist@sensewave.com

Kinsarvik
PO Box 73, 5782 Kinsarvik
☎ 53 66 31 12
www.ullensvang.herad.no

Kvam
5610 Øystese
☎ 56 55 59 10
www.kvam-reiselivskontor.no

Kvam
5600 Norheimsund
☎ 56 55 15 85
e-mail: k-reise@online.no

Lofthus
☎ 53 66 11 90
e-mail: turistinfo@lofthus.no

Odda
Opheimsvegen 31, 5750 Odda
☎ 53 65 40 05
www.visitodda.com

Røldal
5760 Røldal
☎ 53 64 20 33
www.roldal.no

Utne
☎ 53 66 18 22

Ulvik
5730 Ulvik
☎ 56 52 63 60
www.visit.ulvik.com

Agatunet
5776 Stiftelsen Agatunet
☎ 53 66 22 14
E-mail: agatunet@online.no
A collection of over 30 properties,
the oldest dating from c. AD1250.

Granvin Bygdetun
☎ 56 52 40 00
The old village square (Bygdetun)
includes an eighteenth century
house, Holvenstova. A museum
on the ground floor features over
1,000 objects from local
community life.

Hardanger Folkemuseum
Utne
☎ 53 67 00 40
The regional museum for the
fjord.

Hardanger Fartøyvernsenter
Norheimsund
☎ 56 55 33 50
www.fartoyvern.no
Boatbuilding museum, film
presentation, café, rowing boat
hire, fjord tours. Open June–
August, 10am–5pm.

Ingebrigt Vik Museum, Øystese
Contains works by Ingebrigt, one of
Norway's greatest sculptors. Also
features works by other Norwegian
artists. ☎ 56 55 30 00

Kvam Museum, The Rectory
Vikøy
☎ 56 55 30 00
Adolph Tidemand, the Norwegian
artist, stayed here several times.
Open Wednesdays, mid-June to
mid-August, noon-6pm.

Above: Baroniet Rosendal.

Baroniet Rosendal
Postboks 235, 5486 Rosedal
☎ 53 48 29 99
www.baroniet.no
Open early May to mid-September
from 11am (closing time varies).
Rest of year, tours by appointment
only.

Left: Hardanger
Fartøyvernsenter,
Boatbuilding museum

ACCOMMODATION

Hotels and Guest Houses

There are international hotels in all the main cities but even in the countryside there are small hotels. Many of the hotel chains operate voucher schemes which are paid for in advance, giving up to a 50 per cent discount on accommodation. More than 200 hotels participate in the Fjord Pass which gives 20 per cent discounts for two adults and children under 15 between the beginning of May and the end of September. See www.fjordpass.no.

Best Western and its associate hotels have their Travel Card which offers significant summer savings.

Mountain hotels are a Norwegian speciality offering all facilities and providing an excellent base for walking holidays. Local tourist offices can provide addresses of private homes taking in guests.

All hotels offer reduced rates in summer. The majority of establishments allow children under 3 to stay in their parents' room for a quarter of the price, and those up to 12, or sometimes 15, for half price. Guest houses in Norway are called *Pensjonat* or *gjestehus*, and are cheaper.

There are also a number of pass schemes, giving considerable reductions. Leaflets called the *Scandinavian Bonus Pass*, *Fjord-Pass* and *Hotelcheque Scandinavia* are available from the Norwegian National Tourist Office. A card may be purchased at modest cost, giving discounts to two adults and any children under 15 at participating hotels.

The Norwegian Tourist Board can supply a list of all hotels, motels, guest houses and family hostels in Norway, and your local travel agency should be able to provide a booking service. You can also book by post or telephone; practically everyone in Norway speaks English. If travelling in the high season (mid-June to mid-August), it is advisable to book ahead. Local tourist offices in Norway often have a reservation service, charging a small fee. For more information about accommodation visit www.visitnorway.com.

Camping

Camping is allowed almost anywhere provided it is not close to someone's home, or in an area clearly marked as private. It is not permitted to pitch a tent or park a caravan within 500ft/150m of a house/chalet. There are more than a thousand campsites in Norway, most equipped to a very high standard, with hot water and electricity. Sites are usually awarded one, two or three stars, depending on the facilities. There is no standard price and rates do vary. Reservations are not necessary.

Caravans may not be parked on lay-bys or picnic sites. It is forbidden to have an open fire – which includes a camping stove – in forests or on open land between 15 April and 15 September.

The Norwegian Tourist Board publishes an annual guide covering every campsite in Norway, with addresses and telephone numbers, and symbols. For more information visit the Norwegian Hospitality Association website at www.camping.no. Camp sites usually have provision for tents, camper vans (mobile homes), caravans, trailers and many have cabins (hytte) too.

Cabins (*Hytter*)

These are another Norwegian speciality. They can vary from a simple pine cabin consisting of one room to luxury chalets with two or three bedrooms, bathroom, fully fitted kitchens and so on. All provide facilities for cooking as well as crockery, cleaning utensils and detergents. Many appear to have no grills, toasters or a kettle. Towels and bed linen should be taken, although they may be hired at some establishments. Cabins (*hytter*) come in various sizes, but they normally house four to six people. Signposts to the *hytter* can be spotted throughout the main tourist areas. If you are looking for accommodation, ask at the reception desk if they have any vacancies. On some sites you drive round until you see a key in the door of one of the cabins. This means the cabin is available, so take the key to reception and check in. For more information go to www.norgesbooking.no.

If you are interested, get a copy of the free NAF Camping Guide (produced annually) from Norges Automobile Forbund, PB 6682, Etterstad, NO – 0609, Oslo, Norway, ☎ (47) 22 34 14 00. Alternatively, contact your Norwegian Tourist Board.

The more non-perishable foodstuffs you take, the less you will need to purchase in Norway, where it is likely to be more expensive. Even fresh items are likely to be more expensive then you are used to. Demand for the hytte (and other accommodation) is highest during the school holidays. The latter are generally over by mid-August and other Continental families are mostly on their way home by then.

Youth Hostels

To stay in a youth hostel, you must be a member of your own national Youth Hostel Association or you can join in Norway. To find out more contact Norske Vandrerhjem, Dronningensgate 26, N-0154 Oslo 1. www.vandrerhjem.com. All youth hostels mentioned are part of the IYHF (International Youth Hostel Federation).

Farm Stays

Farm holidays are a great way to experience the real Norway and are great value too. Most farms also offer fishing, horse riding and boat rentals. For more information, visit www.nbt-nett.no.

Aurland

Hotel/Motel
Aurland Fjordhotel
☎ 57 63 35 05
post@aurland-fjordhotel.com

Vangsgaarden Motell and Rorbuer Aabelheim Pensjonat
☎ 57 63 35 80 Fax 57 63 35 95
vangsgas@online.no
www.vangsgaarden.no

Camping
NAF Lunde Gard and Camping,
Camping *** hytte ** to ****
Postboks 57, 5741 Aurland
☎ 57 63 34 12   Fax 57 63 31 65
lunde.camping@alb.no

Skresanden Hytter
☎ 57 63 34 72

Winjum Hytter
☎ 57 63 34 61

Youth Hostel
See Flåm

Balestrand Area

Hotel/Motel
Kviknes Hotel
6898 Balestrand
☎ 57 69 42 00
booking@kviknes.no
www.kviknes.no

Camping

NAF Veganeset Camping
Camping *** hytte ** to ****
6899 Balestrand
☎ 57 69 16 12   Fax 57 69 16 12
Veganset.camping@c2i.net
www.vegansetcamping.no

**NAF Solvang Camping,
Hytter and Motell**
Camping **** hytte ** to ****
6894 Vangsnes
☎ 57 69 66 20   Fax 57 69 67 55
Solvang.camping@sognapost.no
www.solvangcamping.com

NOTE on the south side of the fjord
opposite Balestrand

Youth Hostel

Balestrand
6899 Balestrand
☎ 57 69 13 03
www.kringsja.no

Bergen

Hotels and guest houses are plentiful
(listed in free booklets). Also rooms in
private houses are available and all
may be booked through the Tourist
Information Office.

Camping

Two sites on the outskirts of Bergen:
NAF Skogtum Camping
Camping *** hytte** to ****
Skoge, 5357 Fjell
☎ 56 33 48 66   Fax 56 33 63 44
helgnils@online.no
www.skogtun-camping.no

Bratland Camping
Camping **** hytte ** to *****
Bratlandsveien 6, 5268 Haukeland
☎ 55 10 13 38   Fax 55 10 53 60
Post@bratlandcamping.no
www.bratlandcamping.no

Youth Hostel

Bergen Vandrerhjem YMCA
Nedre Korskirkealmenning 4
☎ 55 60 60 55   Fax 55 60 60 51
ymca@online.no
Open all year around, two minutes
from the Fish Market. Private rooms
available.

Eidfjord

Hotel/Motel

Eidfjord Hotel
5783 Eidfjord,
☎ 53 66 52 64
www.post@effh.no

Quality Hotel, Vøringfoss
☎ 53 67 41 00
www. eidfjord-hardanger.no

Fossli Hotel
☎ 53 66 57 77
www.fossli-hotel.com

Guesthouses/Pensions

Eidfjord Gjestgiveri
Øvre Eidfjord
☎ 53 66 53 46
www.ovre-eifjord.com

Vik Pensjonat og Hytter
5783 Eidfjord
☎ 53 66 51 62
www.vikpensjonat.com

Camping

NAF Saebø Camping
Camping ***   hytte ** to ****
5784 Øvre Eidfjord
☎ 53 66 59 27
Scampi@online.no

Garen Camping Gaard & Hyttesenter
☎ 53 66 57 21   Fax 53 66 51 95
Garen.gaard@c2i.net

Geiranger

Hotel/Motel

Hotell Geiranger
6216, Geiranger
☎ 70 26 30 05
Booking@hotel-geiranger.no
www.hotel-geiranger.no

Grande Fjord Hotell
☎ 70 26 94 90   Fax 70 26 94 91

Villa Utsikten
6216 Geiranger
☎ 70 26 96 60
Villa@villautsikten.no
www.villautsikten.no

Camping

NAF Geiranger Camping
Camping ***
6216 Geiramger
☎ 70 26 31 20   Fax 70 26 31 20
Postmaster@geirangercamping.no
www.geirangercamping.no

NAF Geirangerfjorden Feriesenter
Camping ***   hytte ** to ****
6216 Geiranger
☎ 95 10 75 27
fmgrande@online.no
www.geirangerfjorden.net

NAF Vinje Camping
Camping ***   hytte ****
6216 Geiranger
☎ 70 26 30 17   Fax 70 26 30 15
Post@vinje-camping.no
www.vinje-camping.no

Granvin

Guesthouse

Eidestova Guesthouse
Granvin Kai
☎ 56 52 52 51

Camping

Granvin Hytter and Camping
Camping***   hytte** to ***
Kyrkjestrondi, 5736 Granvin
☎ 56 52 52 82
Post@granvin-hytter.no

Espelandsdalen Camping
Camping ***
Espelandsdalen
☎ 56 52 51 67
Post@espelandsdalencamping.no

Gudvangen

Hotel/Motel

Stalheim Hotel
5715 Stalheim
☎ 56 52 01 22   fax 56 52 00 56
Booking@stalheim.com
www.stalheim.com
This hotel is not in Gudvangen village
– see itinerary for details

Gudvangen Fjordtell & Apartments,
5717 Gudvangen
☎ 57 63 39 29   fax 5763 39 80
Fjordtell@online.no
www.gudvangen.com

Camping

NAF Hemre Gard & Camping
Camping ***   hytte ** to ****
5747 Gudvangen
☎ 57 63 39 36   fax 57 63 39 72
Botolf@ctv.es
www. nafcamp.com/hemre-camping

Gudvangen Camping
5747 Gudvangen
☎ 57 63 39 34
j-stee@online.no

Hellesyllt

Hotel/Motel

Grand Hotel
Hellesyllt
☎ 70 26 51 00

Camping

Hellesyllt Touristsenter
6218 Hellesyllt
☎ 90 20 68 85   fax 70 26 52 10
Hellebos@online.no

Youth Hostel

Vandrerhjem
6218 Hellesyllt
☎ 70 26 51 28   fax 70 26 36 57
Hellesyllt.hostel@vandrerhjem.no

Jondal

Cottage/Guest house

Bakketun Overnatting
5628 Herand
☎ 53 66 81 59
m-o-saml@online.no

Svåsand Gardstun
5627, Jondal
☎ 53 66 82 35

Herandsholmen
☎ 53 66 82 30
www.herandsholmen.com

Folgefonn Gjestetun
☎ 53 66 80 55
www.folgefonn-gjestetun.no

Camping

Vassel Gård
5628,Herand. Cabins also.
☎ 53 66 81 78

Folgefonn Hytte-og-Gardscamping,
5627, Jondal. Cabins also.
☎ 53 66 84 23
www.gardscamping.no

Kaupanger

Camping

Amble Gård
6854 Kaupanger
☎ 57 67 81 70
www.amblegaard.no

Timberlids Hytte
6854, Kaupanger
☎ 57 67 87 64
www.timberlid.no

Camping at Amblasanden Bubilcamping
6853, Kaupanger
☎ 57 67 81 70 or 41 24 53 51
www.amblegaard.no

Laerdal

Hotel/Motel

Lindstrøm Hotel
PO Box 114, 6886 Laerdal
☎ 57 66 69 00   Fax 57 66 66 81
post@lindstroemhotel.no

Offerdal Hotell, 6887 Laerdal
☎ 57 66 61 01 Fax 57 66 62 25
granden@online.no
www.offerdal-hotell.no

Camping

The nearest NAF sites are in the
Laerdal Valley:
NAF Bjøraker Camping
Camping ** hytte **
6888 Steinklepp
☎ 57 66 87 20

NAF Borund Hyttesenter og Camping Steinklepp
Camping ** hytte ** to ****
6888 Steinklepp
☎ 57 66 81 71 Fax 57 66 81 71
Ovoldum@online.no
www.hyttesenter.com

Youth Hostel

The nearest youth hostel is 25 miles/
40kms up the valley, near to Borgund
Stave Church.

Borlag Turistheim
6888 Steinklepp
☎ 57 66 87 80 Fax 557 66 87 44
Borrh@online.no

Lom

Camping

Nordal Turistsenter
Camping****hytte** to ****
2656 Lom
☎ 61 21 93 00 Fax 61 21 93 01
Booking@nordalturistsenter.no
www.nordalturistsenter.no

Youth Hostel

The nearest youth hostel is:

Bøverdalen
2687 Bøverdalen
☎ 61 21 20 64 Fax 61 21 20 64
boeverdalen.hostel@vandrerhjem.no

Hotels

Fossberg Hotell
☎ 61 21 22 50 Fax 61 21 22 51
www.fossberg.no
booking@fossberg.no

Fossheim Hotell, 2686 Lom
☎ 61 21 95 00 Fax 61 21 95 01
Resepsjon@fossheimhotel.no
fossheim@fossheimhotel.no
www.fossheimhotel.no

Hotell OG Skysstasjon
2686 Lom
☎ 61 21 20 31 Fax 61 21 21 51
www.roisheim.no

Fact File

Lofthus

Hotel
Hotel Ullensvang
5787 Lofthus I Hardanger
☎ 53 67 00 00
ullensvang@hostel–ullensvang.no
www.hotel–ullensvang.no

Youth Hostel
Hardanger Vandrerhjem
5781 Lofthus
☎ 53 67 14 00
Lofthus.hostel@vandrerhjem.no

Camping
Lofthus Camping
5781 Lofthus. Cabins also.
Indoor swimming pool.
☎ 53 66 13 64
www.lofthuscamping.com

Norheimsund

Camping
Mo Camping
5800 Norheimsund
☎ 56 55 17 27

Oddland Camping
Vikøyvn 396, 5600 Norheimsund
☎ 56 55 16 86
Price includes rowing boats, April-
October only.
www.hardangerfjord.com

Naf Kro & Camping
Postboks 156, 5602 Norheimsund,
Kvamskogen
☎ 56 55 31 31
Facilities for the disabled but 10km
from town.

Odda

Hotel
Hardanger Hotel, Odda
Tel 53 64 64 64
post@hardangerhostel.no

Guest House
Apothekergaarden Gjestehus
☎ 53 64 41 36
www.apothekergaardenengjestehus.com

Camping
NAF Odda Camping Borsta
5750 Odda ***
☎ 53 64 16 10
Post@oppleve.no
www.oppleve.no

Hildal Camping
Tel 53 64 50 36

Odda Hytte–OG Gjestegård
☎ 53 64 23 27

Øystese

Hotel
Hardangerfjord Hotel
☎ 56 55 63 00
www.hardangerfjord-hotell.no

Camping
Hardanger Fjordhytter
Hardangerfjordwegen 800, 5610
Øystese
☎ 56 55 51 80
www.hardanger-fjordhytter.no

Skei

Camping
Hoyseth Turiststasjon & Camping
6843 Skei i Jølster
☎ 57 72 89 63

Sogndal

Camping
Kjørnes Camping
Camping **** hytte ** to ****
6856 Sogndal
☎ 57 67 45 80 Fax 57 67 33 26
Camping@kjornes.no
www.kjornes.no

Stedje Camping
Pb.1., N-6851 Sogndal
☎ 90 07 10 12
Post@scamping.no

Youth Hostel
Sogndal Youth Hostel
Helgheimsvegan 9, 6856 Sogndal
☎ 57 62 75 75 Fax 57 62 75 70
Sogndalhostel@vandrerhjem.no

Stryn

Hotel
Visnes Hotel
Prestestegen 1, Postboks 1, 6781 Stryn
☎ 57 87 10 87 Fax 57 87 20 75
booking@visnes.no
www.visnes.no

Guest House
Vesla Pensjonat
Stryn
☎ 57 87 10 06
www.veslapensjon.no

Camping
Naf Stryn Camping
Camping**** hytte** to ****
Bøaveien 6, Postboks 57, 6781 Stryn
☎ 57 87 11 36 Fax 57 87 20 25
stryn-c@online.no
www.stryn-camping.no

Lo-vik Camping
Camping**** hytte*** to ****
6789 Loen
☎ 57 87 76 19 Fax 57 87 78 11

Løken Camping
Postboks 95, 6784 Olden
☎ 57 87 32 68 Fax 57 87 30 05

Youth Hostel
Stryn Youth Hostel
geileveien 14, 6783 Stryn
☎ 57 87 11 06 Fax 57 87 20 81
Stryn.hostel@vandrerhjem.no

Ulvik

Hotel
Rica Brakanes Hotel
☎ 56 52 61 05
www.brakanes-hotel.no

Ulvik Fjord Pensjonat
☎ 56 52 61 70
www.ulvikfjord.no

Camping
Oydvinstod Hyttegrend
☎ 90 83 14 97
www.oydvinstod.no

AIRLINES

SAS
☎ 0870 6072 7727

Norwegian
☎ 47 21 49 00 15

British Airways
☎ 0845 7733377

British Midland Airways
☎ 0870 6070555

Ryanair
☎ 0871 2460 000

Arrivals and Customs

Norway operates red and green channels for customs – red for something to declare, and green for nothing to declare. Because of the strict drinking laws, you might be stopped on entry and asked what drink you have bought. Travellers aged 20 and over are allowed to take 1 litre of spirits and 1 litre of wine or fortified wine into Norway. If no spirits are taken, the allowance is 2 litres of wine and fortified wines. In addition, 2 litres of beer are allowed. People aged 16 and over can also take in 200 cigarettes or 250g of other tobacco. Additional alcohol may be taken in, but it will be taxed and the extra duty on fortified wine, sparkling wine and spirits is very high.

There are very strict rules banning the importation of a wide range of agricultural produce, including meat, fruit and berries, in order to prevent the spread of plant and animal diseases. It is also prohibited to bring in eggs and potatoes, milk and cream from non-Scandinavian countries, mammals, birds, plants for cultivation, drugs, medicines, weapons and ammunition. Small quantities of medicines for personal use are exempt, as are small bunches of flowers or pot plants intended as gifts.

Customs posts between Norway and Sweden are often unmanned. UK visitors need a valid passport but there are no visa requirements unless you are planning a long stay, or intend working. Other nationals should consult the Norwegian embassy or consulate.

BANKS

All towns and most large villages have one or more banks which will exchange currency. Some will also exchange cash against major credit cards. Banks are usually open between 8.15am and 3pm during the week, with an extension on Thursdays to 5pm. Branches in rural areas may have shorter opening hours. There are usually facilities to exchange currency at airports and ports, and in most hotels.

BICYCLES

Bikes can often be hired from hotels, campsites, local tourist offices and sports shops, as well as cycle-hire stores in the larger towns. A number of companies also offer special cycling tours.

CHEMISTS/DRUGSTORES

Pharmacies are called *Apotek* and open during normal shopping hours, with some operating an emergency duty at night and weekends.

There are strict controls on drugs and strong medicines are available only through a chemist, usually on prescription. Mild painkillers and insect bite creams can be bought in general stores.

CURRENCY AND CREDIT CARDS

The currency is the Norwegian Krone which is usually written as Nkr or NOK. The krone consists of 100 Øre. Coins are 10 and 50 Øre, as well as 1, 5 and 10 kroner pieces. Notes are 50, 100, 500 and 1000 NOK. Foreign currency and travellers' cheques can be exchanged at banks and hotels and most adopt a standard exchange rate. Travellers entering the country are allowed to bring in an unlimited amount of foreign currency but are not allowed to take out more than they had on arrival, or more than 5,000 NOK in notes and coins. Filling stations do not accept travellers' cheques. All major credit cards are generally accepted in hotels, stores and restaurants; cash may be preferred in isolated areas.

DRIVING

Breakdown

Help from Norway's motor rescue patrols – Norges Automobilforbund (NAF) – is free to members of the RAC, AA, and the American AAA. NAF patrols cover all the major roads and mountain passes during the peak holiday periods. There are also NAF emergency phones in many mountain areas.

If more extensive repair work is required you will have to pay for any tow-in and garage charges. There is a very efficient system of moving spare parts around the country, often using overnight mail trains, so even major breakdowns can be tackled quite quickly. You must carry a red warning triangle in the event of a breakdown.

Caravans

Caravans are not suitable for use on some roads, and a free map available from the Norwegian Tourist Board indicates which routes can be taken, permitted axle loads, permitted length of vehicles, roads open to caravans, and tunnels. Cars towing caravans must be fitted with large caravan mirrors, which should be folded or removed when the caravan is not on tow. The maximum speed limit for a caravan with brakes is 80kph/50mph, or 60kph/37mph if it weighs more than 300kg and has no brakes. Touring caravans 2.3m wide are allowed, and may be up to 2.5m wide provided the towing vehicle is at least the same width. The length of car and caravan must not exceed 18.5m.

Norwegian roads are well signposted and most towns and villages have an information board in a convenient lay-by with information on the local tourist office, hotels or campsites, and places of interest.

Car rental

Car rental is available in most towns and larger villages, as well as at all major airports and ports. Drivers must be aged 21 years or over, have a valid driving licence and some form of identification. A major credit card is the preferred form of payment. Many of the car hire companies offer special deals at certain times of the year and it pays to shop around.

Driving Regulations

A valid driving licence is required for driving in Norway and it is prudent to have the vehicle's documents with you and check that your insurance affords full cover. Foreign cars must carry the appropriate country identification sticker.

The Norwegians drive on the right-hand side of the road and on dual carriageways the left-hand lane is reserved for overtaking vehicles. A yellow warning line means that it is not safe to overtake and it is illegal to cross a continuous line.

Speed limits are well signposted. They are generally 50kph/30mph in built-up areas, falling to 30kph/20mph in some residential areas. Top speed outside built-up areas is 80kph/50mph except on some better stretches of road, where signs indicate it is increased to 90kph/55mph. Cars towing caravans or trailers are still restricted to 80kph/50mph even in a 90kph/55mph area.

It is compulsory to wear seat belts in both front and back (if fitted), and children under the age of four must have their own safety seat. It is also compulsory to drive on dipped headlights during daylight hours, and this rule also applies to motorcycles and mopeds, whose drivers and passengers must wear crash helmets. Cars from the UK must have the headlights adjusted so that they don't dazzle oncoming traffic in Norway.

The Norwegian drink-drive laws are very tough. The alcohol limit is 0.05% and if you plan to drive it is best not to drink alcohol at all. It is also a serious offence to drive while under the influence of drugs, and this could include some prescribed medicines. In Norway medicines containing drugs which should be avoided when driving are marked with a red triangle.

Heavy vehicles are not allowed on some roads and a map showing permitted axle weights on Norwegian roads can be obtained free from tourist offices.

Fuel

In towns and cities filling stations are numerous but they are not so common in rural areas. Never let the tank get too low and always fill up when you have the opportunity. Many garages in the country only accept cash. Diesel oil and unleaded petrol are available.

Motorways

There are only motorways in the south-east although the major roads travelling north allow you to keep up a steady speed. There are two types of motorway – Motorvei Klass A and Motorvei Klass B. The first is a two-lane dual carriageway, while the second is a two-lane road from 7–8m (20–25 feet) wide with limited access points. Maximum speed on a motorway is 90kph/55mph.

Traffic coming in from the right usually has priority. Red flow signs indicate that traffic entering from the right must be allowed to filter in.

Mountain Driving

This requires a great deal of concentration, especially on the smaller roads which can be quite narrow. Often these roads are only wide enough for a single lane of traffic although there are numerous passing points. These may be indicated by a sign with a white M on a blue background. The rule for mountain driving is take your time. Generally the Norwegians are courteous drivers and will drop back and wait until safe to pass rather than pressure you into driving faster.

Elk signs are a warning to exercise greater vigilance, especially at night. Elk are large creatures and a collision with one can write a car off. Not all mountain passes are open all year round and if you are travelling in spring or autumn, it is vital to check before setting out on your journey.

Parking

Parking is not allowed on main roads, on bends or in blind spots. Towns and cities may have their own parking regulations forbidding parking on particular sides of the street on some days.

Tolls

Tolls are charged on a number of roads in Norway. There are also a number of private bridges and roads on which tolls are levied, although these are not part of the public highway network. Many of these private toll bridges and roads operate an 'honesty box' system, with a sign telling you how much you have to pay. Tolls on public roads vary from a few kroner to 30 or 40 kroner. Tolls (15 kroner) are being levied on all drivers travelling into Oslo in a bid to reduce the city's traffic congestion.

Tunnels

Norway has some of the longest tunnels in Europe, many blasted through the mountains. Some of these are none too wide and care must be exercised. The country's longest tunnel is the Svartistunnelen on the R17 in Nordland which is 7.5km (4 miles) long. There are nine other tunnels which are all more than 4.5 km (2.5 miles) long.

Useful Road Signs

ferist – cattle grid, *veiarbeide* – roadworks, *kjør sakte* – drive slowly, *løs grus* – loose chippings, *omkjøring* – diversion, *svake kanter* – soft verges.

Winter Travel

It is illegal to drive in snow or ice with summer tyres without chains. Many drivers use studded tyres and these can be hired from Ulrich Gummiservice, Drammensveien 130, N-0277 Oslo 2, ☎ (02) 55 77 18. It is not permitted to use studded tyres between 15 April and 1 November (or in the north from 1 May to 15 October) unless you are specifically going into areas of ice and snow.

ELECTRICITY

Electricity operates at 220 volts AC. Round-ended, two-pronged continental adaptors are needed for UK appliances.

NOTE: Some ferries and coastal steamers have 220V DC electrical supplies and this could damage electric razors, hairdryers etc.

EMBASSIES AND CONSULATES

The main embassies and consulates are:

Australian Consulate
Wilh. Wilhelmsen ASA
Strandvn 20
Lysaker
☎ 67 58 48 48

UK
British Embassy
Thomas Heftyesgate 8
0265 Oslo
☎ 22 55 24 00

Canada
Wergelandsveien 7
Oslo
☎ 22 99 53 00

USA
United States Embassy
Drammensveien 18
Oslo 2
☎ 22 44 85 50

Norwegian Embassies Overseas

UK
Royal Norwegian Embassy
25 Belgrave Square
London SW1 8QD
☎ 020 7591 5500

USA
Royal Norwegian Embassy
2720 34th Street NW
Washington DC
20008 USA
☎ (0101) 202 333 6000

EMERGENCY NUMBERS

110 Fire   112 Police   113 Ambulance

FACILITIES FOR THE DISABLED

Disabled people are generally well catered for in Norway. By law, all public buildings must be accessible to disabled people. Many trains have special facilities for the disabled, including hydraulic lifts for people boarding in wheelchairs. The Norwegian Association for the Handicapped publishes the *Travel Guide for the Disabled* (in English). This 192-page comprehensive survey includes transport facilities, accommodation and points of interest which are especially accessible for disabled persons. You can obtain a copy from the Norwegian Tourist Board, or Norges Handikapforbund, PO Box 9217 Vaterland, N-0134 Oslo.

FERRIES

Color Lines operate between Germany, Denmark, Sweden and Norway. www.colorline.no.

DFDS operates year round between Norway, Sweden, Denmark and England. www.seaeurope.com.

Fact File

Fjord Line operates all year round between England, Denmark and Western Norway. www.fjordline.com.

Stena Line operates between Denmark and Norway. www.stenaline.no.

Ferry timetables

A summary of all major routes in Norway including ferry connections is published by the Norwegian Tourist Board. A complete Internal Timetable with full schedules and fares for all bus, train, air and boat services – *Rutebok for Norge* – is published five times a year. It has explanations in English and contains all relevant telephone numbers and addresses, and is an invaluable planning aid. Check with the tourist board for current price.

HEALTH INSURANCE

Because of reciprocal agreements, UK citizens can receive free medical care while in Norway although a charge may be made for some specialised services, which can often be reclaimed when you return home. An E111 form is needed to be eligible for this and the forms are obtainable from post offices. Other nationals should ensure they have adequate travel and health insurance before leaving home.

MAPS

Good road maps can be bought at stationers, bookshops and many garages. Walking maps and guides can be bought at tourist offices, hotels, hostels and bookshops. Regional and municipal tourist offices can often provide street maps and local maps. The following maps are useful: Cappelens Road Hiking and Survey maps of Norway 1:325,000; Hallwag Map of Norway 1:1,000,000; Norwegian Highway Authority (Norske Vegkart) 1:250,000 (21 maps covering the whole country); Norway Insight Travel Map. If you have difficulty then contact the map specialists Stanfords, 12–14 Long Acre, Covent Garden, London WC2E 9LP. ☎ 020 7836 0189; www.stanfords.co.uk.

MEASUREMENTS

The metric system is used in Norway. Conversions are:
1 kilogram (1,000 grams) = 2.2lb; 1 litre = 1.76 pints; 4.5 litres = 1 gallon; 8km = 5 miles

MEDICAL TREATMENT

This can be obtained from doctors' and dentists' surgeries during treatment hours, or from hospital casualty wards outside these times. Most hotels have doctors on call and will put you in touch with one in an emergency. Doctors and dentists are paid cash which is reclaimed by medical insurance or reciprocal health agreements. Ambulance travel and hospital in-patient treatment is free, as are tooth extractions. Most communities have first aid stations (*lelevakt*) for minor injuries.

Some charges may be partially refunded by Norway's social insurance scheme. Obtain a receipt for payment and claim at the district social insurance office called *trygdekontor*.

POST OFFICES

Usually open Monday to Friday at either 8am or 8.30am and close at 4pm or 5pm and open Saturday 8am to 1pm.

PUBLIC HOLIDAYS

New Year's Day; Maundy Thursday; Good Friday; Easter; Easter Monday; May Day; Constitution Day; Ascension Day; Whit Monday; Christmas Day and Boxing Day

There are also a number of flag days. These celebrate religious festivals, important dates in the country's history, and the birthdays of members of the royal family. These are:

New Year's Day; 21 February (birthday of Crown Prince Harald); Easter; May Day; 8 May (Liberation Day, 1945); 17 May (Constitution Day); Whit Monday; 7 June (Dissolution of the Union 1905); 2 July (birthday of King Olav); 4 July (birthday of Crown Princess Sonja); 20 July (birthday of Prince Haakon Magnus); 29 July (St Olav's Day); 22 September (birthday of Princess Maertha Louise); Christmas Day

SHOPPING

In most towns and cities the larger shops open Monday to Wednesday from 9am to 5pm and stay open till 7pm on Thursday and Friday. On Saturday they open from 9am to 3pm.

State alcohol shops are open Monday to Wednesday 10am–4pm, Thursday 10am–5pm, Friday 9am–4pm, and Saturday 9am–1pm. In the summer months of June to August some shops may operate shorter opening hours. There is a returnable deposit on all bottles of wine bottled in Norway.

Tax-Free Shopping

This is available in stores throughout Norway which can be recognised by stickers in their windows. At least 300 NOK must be spent to qualify for the VAT refund. Goods purchased must not be used in Norway and must be taken out of the country within four weeks of purchase. Tax-free shopping is not available to Scandinavian nationals and a passport is needed as proof of residence. The receipt will have to be produced at the airport, ferry port or station before you leave, in order to claim back the VAT.

Shopping is expensive but items worth considering are knitwear, pewterware, silver jewellery, wooden carvings, reindeer goods, and food and fish.

SMOKING

This is banned in all public buildings, and on domestic air routes.

SPORTS

Canoeing

Only the most experienced canoers should venture into the open sea. The Telemark Canal (Telemarkskanalen) runs from Dalen, where canoes can be hired, for 110km (70 miles) to Skien. There are eighteen locks, many of them

Fact File

close to waterfalls which should always be approached with great caution.

For further information contact the canoeing association: Norges Padelforbund, Service boks 1, Ullevål Stadium, 0840 Oslo, ☎ 47 21 02 98 35.

Cycling

The National Cyclists' Association (Syklistenes Landesforening, Youngstorget, Storgt 23D, 0028 Oslo, ☎ 22 47 30 30) produces a map with twenty-two suggested routes covering the whole country. All the routes are linked so that you can move from one to another if you have time. The map also shows which roads are not suitable for cyclists, usually because of tunnels from which cyclists are banned. Good lights are essential because not all tunnels are illuminated, and where access to cyclists is barred, diversion signs indicate the route to follow.

Cycles can be carried on all trains except express trains and there is a charge. You must arrive at the station at least 30 minutes before departure, and the cycle must carry a label with name, address and places of destination and departure.

Buses in rural areas have provision for carrying bikes but space is limited. They are carried on ferries free of charge.

Diving

The warm waters of the Gulf Stream which flow around Norway provide excellent conditions for underwater exploration. You can get more information about dive operators on www.visitnorway.com. For diving in the Arctic Barents Sea go to www.arctic-dive.no.

Fishing

Fishing licences are readily available locally from sports suppliers, kiosks, tourist offices, hotels, campsites, etc. and can be either for one stretch of water or a collection of lakes and rivers. They can cover a day, a week or a season and the price depends on duration and the quality of the fishing. As a rule, a separate licence is needed for net or otter fishing. To protect the fisheries, all equipment brought into the country must be disinfected.

A licence is not needed for sea fishing although the inland regulations and conservation measures regarding salmon, trout and sea char also apply at sea. National fishing licences can by bought at local post offices.

Fishing seasons vary from district to district – ask at the local tourist board, get in touch with the regional *lensman* (county sheriff), or contact the Directorate for Wildlife Administration (Direktoratet for naturforvaltning), Tungsletta 2, N-7000 Trondheim.

Golf

Golf is played from May to September and there are courses in Oslo, Blommenholm, Kolbotn, Sarpsborg, Borgenhaugen, Fredrikstad, Hov, Røyken, Trønsberg, Skien, Arendal, Kristiansand, Stavanger, Bergen and Trondheim. Guest or day membership can be arranged and clubs can be hired. Contact the Golf Association for a list of golf courses at Norges Golfforbund: ☎ 22 73 66 20 or email golfforbundet@nif.idrett.no.

Horse Riding

There are many riding stables and a number of farms also hire out horses which can be hired for a short period or a full day, or you can set out on organised tours lasting a week or more. There are more than forty horse riding establishments throughout Norway offering everything from gentle day rides to week-long ride-camp expeditions. For further information see www.visitnorway.com.

Mountaineering

There are many ranges and peaks to explore, especially in the north with the Lofoten and Vesterålen mountains and the ranges on the Lyngen peninsula in Troms. The Norwegian Mountain Touring Association (DNT), PO Box 7 Sentrum, 0101 Oslo, ☎ 22 82 28 00, organises the sport and arranges courses and expeditions.

Skiing

There are excellent winter downhill and cross-country facilities in many areas, and it is possible to ski during the summer in Oppland, Hordaland, Sogn og Fjordane and Nordland The summer skiing season lasts as a general rule from June to September. For information contact Skiforeningen (Ski Society), Kongeveien 5, 0787 Oslo. ☎ 22 92 32 00. www.skiforeningen.no.

Swimming

Swimming is possible almost anywhere, but the water may be cold. The inland lakes and their islands provide very safe bathing. Even above the Arctic Circle it is possible to swim in the lakes on very hot days and after a hot spell the water temperature can be acceptable. Official bathing sites are usually clearly marked. There are many swimming pools run by hotels and municipalities.

Walking

There are hundreds of miles of well-marked trails in and around Oslo, and every community can give you details of walks in its area. Tourist offices often have guides to walks in their districts which contain details of things to see along the way, the time to be taken and the difficulty of the terrain.

There are many guided walks, especially on the mountains and across glaciers. Glacier walking, however, should never be attempted without an experienced local guide. During summer organised glacier walks take place daily from the Leirvassbu, Glitterheim, Spiterstulen, Juvasshytta, Krossbu and Sognefjell mountain touring huts.

Mountain maps can be obtained from the Mountain Touring Association (Den Norske Turistforening). If going into the mountains you must be fit, have the right equipment and know how to use it, check the weather forecast and make sure someone knows where you are going and when you plan to return.

Den Norske Turistforening works closely with local mountaineering clubs and together they run a network of 286 cabins and hostels, ranging in size from just four beds to more than a hundred. They are generally open from mid-February to the end of September. There are three types of hostel: serviced hostels with full board (S), self-service cabins with groceries on sale (SS), and unserviced cabins where you have to carry in everything you need (NS). You have to be a DNT member to use the cabins, or be accompanied by one, and must provide your own sheet sleeping bag or sleeping bag. The cabins are all linked by paths which are easy to follow and usually marked by a red 'T'.

Information about DNT and how to join can be obtained from Den Norske Turistforening, Postboks 7 Sentrum, 0101 Oslo, ☎ 22 82 28 00. www.turistforening.no.

TAXIS

Taxis (*drosje*) can be hailed in towns and cities but may need to be booked in advance in rural areas and at night. Fares are reasonable although there are supplements for nights and weekends. Taxis generally accept a tip of 10 per cent and all accept major credit cards.

TELEPHONES

A telephone call from your hotel room is convenient but can be expensive. There are coin-operated telephone boxes in most hotels, restaurants, shops, garages, airports, railway and bus stations, and you can direct dial long distance and overseas provided you have a pocketful of 5 and 10 kroner coins. You can also dial the overseas operator and ask for a reverse charge (collect) call or to make a credit card call. It can take some time to get through to the international operator at certain times of the day, especially if you are ringing from a country area. It is also not unknown for call boxes in outlying areas to be out of order.

To direct dial to the UK from Norway, put the money in the box before dialling 095 44 and then your STD code (omitting the initial zero) and number. For the USA, dial 095 1 followed by the national dialling code for your local exchange, omitting the first zero, and then the number. A meter shows how much credit is left.

To ring Norway from the UK dial 00 47 followed by the town code (omitting the first zero) and then the number. From the USA first dial 011 47.

TOURIST OFFICES

The main Norwegian tourist offices are:

UK
Norwegian National Tourist Office
Charles House
5 Lower Regent Street
London SW1Y 4LR
☎ 020 7839 6255

USA and Canada
Norwegian Tourist Board
655 Third Avenue
New York, USA
NY 10017
☎ (212) 949 1333

Norway
Norwegian Tourist Board
Stortorvet 10
N-0155 Oslo
☎ 24 14 46 00
www.visitnorway.no
e-mail: norway@ntr.no

In the summer season May-September:

Årdal
Tourist Information
Post Box 126, 6881 Årdalstangen
☎ 57 66 35 62
ardalaa@online.no
www.ardal.no

Aurland
5745 Aurland
☎ 57 63 33 13 Fax: 57 63 11 48
info@alr.no
www.air.no

Balestrand
6899 Balestrand
☎ 57 69 12 55

Byrkjelo
6826 Byrkjelo
☎ 57 86 73 01
E-mail: mail@nordfjord.no
www.nordfjord.no

Flåm
Post box 86, 5742 Flåm
☎ 57 63 21 06 Fax: 57 63 11 48
info@air.no
www.air.no

Florø
Tourist Information
Strandgata 30, N-6900, Florø
☎ 57 74 75 05 Fax: 57 74 77 16

Fact File

Fjaerland
6848 Fjaerland
☎ 57 69 32 33 Fax: 57 69 32 11

Gaupne
Infokiosk, 6868 Gaupne
☎ 57 68 15 88
postmaster@lustertourist.com
www.lustertourist.com

Geiranger
Gamle fergekai, NO-6216 Geiranger
☎ 70 26 30 99 Fax: 70 26 57 20
info@visitgeirangerfjorden.com

Hafslo
Hafslo Servicesenter
☎ 57 68 45 85
postermaster@lustertourist.com

Hardanger see page 93

Hellesylt
Samfunnshuset
NO-6218 Hellesylt
☎ 94 81 13 321
hellesylt@dgt.no

Jostedal
Breheimsenteret Jostedal, 6871
Jostedal
☎ 57 68 32 50
www.jostedal.com

Laerdal
Øyrapl. 7, 6887 Laerdal
☎ 57 64 12 07 Fax: 57 66 64 22
info.laerdal@air.no
www.air.no

Lom
Tourist Information
2656 Lom
☎ 61 21 93 00 Fax: 61 21 93 01
booking@nordalturistsenter.no
www.nordalturistsenter.no

Luster
Pyranidensenter, 6868 Gaupne
☎ 97 60 04 43

Naustdal
Tourist Information
Naustdal Kommune, N–6817,
Naustdal
☎ 57 81 61 00

Sandnes
Tourist Information
Vågsgt 22, N–4306
☎ 51 97 55 55 Fax: 51 62 82 14
info@RegionStavanger.com

Skei
6843 Skei I Jølster
☎ 57 72 85 88 Fax: 57 72 19 55
post@sunnfjord.no
www.sunnfjord.no

Skjolden
Fjordstova, 5837 Skjolden
☎ 97 60 04 43
www.lustertourist.com

Sogndal
Sognefjorden AS
Sogndal Kulturhus, Hoven 2
☎ 97 60 04 43
sogndal@sognefjorden.no
www.sognefjorden.no

Stavanger
Tourist Information
Domkirkeplassen 3, N–4006,
Stavanger
☎ 51 85 92 00 Fax: 47 51 85 92 02
info@RegionStavanger.com

Stranda
Kaihuset, NO-6200 Stranda
☎ 70 26 04 00 stranda@dgt.no

Stryn
Tinggt. 3, 6783 Stryn
☎ 57 87 40 40 Fax: 57 87 40 41
mail@nordfjord.no
www.nordfjord.no

Valldal
Open all year round
Sylte, NO-6210 Valldal
☎ 70 25 77 67 Fax: 70 25 70 44
valldal@visitgeirangerfjorden.com

Vik
6893 Vik I Sogn
☎ 57 69 56 86
www.sognefjord.no

Internet
info@sognefjord.no
www.sognefjord.no

Index